The Architectural University

A Developmental Framework For Ethical and Intentional AI Integration in Higher Education

The Architectural University:

A Developmental Framework For Ethical and Intentional AI Integration in Higher Education

RICK

UPCHURCH

TOOLS TO LEAD
Leading people effectively

Published by Tools to Lead Publishing

https://ToolstoLead.com

ISBN: 978-0-9833239-9-0

First Edition

This book is intended for educational and informational purposes. The views expressed are those of the author and do not necessarily reflect the official position of any organization with which the author may be affiliated.

Contents

Preface

This book began in a faculty workshop.

I had been invited to facilitate a professional development session on artificial intelligence at a small liberal arts university. Everyone in that room cared about their students. No one was working from a common framework.

That workshop crystallized what I had been observing for months: the problem was not faculty indifference or technological anxiety. The problem was the absence of a shared architectural vocabulary. Faculty were making course-level decisions in an institutional vacuum. Students were navigating contradictory expectations from one course to another, often within the same semester.

The central argument of this book is straightforward: AI integration in higher education is not a technological decision. It is a curricular architecture decision. Institutions that treat it as the former will perpetually react to the next tool release. Institutions that treat it as the latter will build something that can adapt as tools evolve — because the architecture is grounded in pedagogy, not software.

The framework developed in these pages ultimately points beyond artificial intelligence itself toward a broader vision of educational design—what I will later describe as **the Architectural University**.

I have written this book for the faculty member who wants to redesign a single course responsibly and does not know where to start. I have written it for the dean who needs a shared institutional framework that respects faculty autonomy while creating coherence. I have written it for the instructional designer who sits between faculty intention and course execution and needs language that bridges both worlds. Each of these readers will find a different entry point into this material, and each will, I hope, find something worth using immediately.

A word about what this book does not do. It does not advocate for maximum AI integration. Level 0 – AI Restricted or Prohibited – is not a failure of imagination. It is, in the right course at the right developmental moment, the most pedagogically sound choice available. The framework presented here holds all seven levels with equal seriousness. Architecture means fitting the right structure to the right purpose, not always building higher.

This book also does not pretend that AI integration is without risk. The risks are real – to academic integrity, intellectual formation, equity, and institutional coherence. But risk is an argument for design, not avoidance. The chapters that follow take those risks seriously and offer structured responses to each.

Higher education has always been asked to absorb transformative technologies without losing its essential character: the cultivation of disciplined, ethical, and intellectually courageous human beings. That task has not changed. Only the tools have.

A Note on the Preparation of This Manuscript

Portions of this book were developed in collaboration with an AI writing assistant. That collaboration included drafting and expanding chapter sections, generating extended case studies and appendix templates, and producing structural frameworks for review and revision. In each instance, the intellectual architecture of the work – the arguments, the framework, the evaluative judgments, and the disciplinary claims – originated with the author. AI-generated drafts were reviewed, substantially revised, and in many cases rewritten to reflect the author's own analysis, institutional experience, and scholarly judgment.

No AI-generated content was incorporated without critical evaluation and deliberate editorial decision. This manuscript was written in the spirit of the framework it describes: AI as a collaborative tool within a human-directed intellectual process, with authorship, responsibility, and evaluative authority retained by the human author throughout. The decision to disclose this collaboration here — rather than in a footnote, an acknowledgment, or not at all — is itself an application of the transparency principles this book advances.

A Note on Terminology

Throughout this book, the term artificial intelligence refers primarily to generative AI systems — large language models, image generators, AI-assisted writing and coding tools, and related technologies — as these are the tools most immediately affecting course design decisions in higher education at the time of writing. The arguments and frameworks presented here are intentionally durable: they are grounded in pedagogical principles rather than specific tools, and they are designed to remain applicable as the specific landscape of available AI systems continues to evolve.

When this book uses the term architecture, it means something specific: the intentional alignment of course design, learning outcomes, assessment practices, and institutional policy toward a coherent educational purpose. Architecture is the opposite of reaction. It is the difference between a curriculum shaped by deliberate decisions and one shaped by whatever happened to be available or convenient at the time.

That distinction — between reaction and architecture — is what this entire book is about.

Companion Resources

The complete implementation toolkit—including editable planning templates, the C.L.E.A.R. Design Audit, sample policies, downloadable worksheets, and future updates—is available at:

AI-CAM Integration Planning Templates: https://tinyurl.com/2crtay2q

CLEAR Design Audit: https://tinyurl.com/2crtay2q

Part I. Foundations for AI Integration in Higher Education

Chapter 1: The Imperative for Structured AI Integration

Artificial intelligence is no longer peripheral to higher education. It is embedded in research platforms, writing environments, productivity software, data analytics systems, and professional workflows across nearly every discipline. Students now encounter AI as a functional reality shaping how information is gathered, synthesized, and communicated. The question facing higher education is, therefore, not whether artificial intelligence will influence academic work. It already does. The decisive question is whether institutions will respond to this transformation reactively or architecturally.

AI literacy is no longer optional in higher education; it is a structural responsibility. Yet responses to AI across higher education remain inconsistent. Some instructors prohibit its use entirely. Others permit it without clear boundaries. Still others integrate AI tools informally without embedding them in course design or learning outcomes.

This variability produces confusion, uneven skill development, and fragmented institutional identity. Students navigate contradictory expectations from course to course. Faculty operate without a shared vocabulary. Policies lag behind practice.

Such fragmentation is not merely an administrative inconvenience. It undermines academic coherence.

Defining AI Literacy in an Academic Context

Before institutions can design responsible integration, they must define the competency at stake. In this volume, AI literacy refers to the disciplined ability to evaluate, supervise, and ethically integrate artificial intelligence systems in accordance with disciplinary standards. It includes:

• Conceptual understanding of how generative systems function.
• Critical evaluation of outputs for accuracy, bias, and limitations.
• Transparent disclosure and ethical use.
• The ability to integrate AI assistance without surrendering intellectual agency.

AI literacy is best understood as a metacognitive competency, not mere tool proficiency. Just as information literacy required students to assess source credibility in the digital age, AI literacy requires students to assess system-generated content within disciplinary frameworks.

Graduates entering law, business, healthcare, engineering, education, ministry, and the humanities will be expected not only to use AI tools but to supervise and interpret them. Professionals increasingly operate in environments where AI systems generate drafts, simulate models, recommend strategies, or summarize data. The value of the human professional lies not in competing with automation, but in exercising judgment over it.

If institutions do not intentionally cultivate this competency, students will still use AI. They will simply do so without shared norms, structured formation, or critical discipline. The result is uneven development; some students become sophisticated evaluators, while others become dependent users. Both outcomes weaken institutional responsibility.

The Risk of Unstructured Adoption

Rapid technological diffusion invites reactive responses. In the absence of coherent frameworks, AI adoption often occurs informally. Faculty members experiment independently. Students discover tools through social media. Institutional policy trails implementation that has already begun. Unstructured adoption introduces at least four significant risks.

First, foundational skill erosion. If students prematurely outsource cognitive processes, such as drafting arguments, synthesizing research, or solving foundational problems, to AI without first mastering underlying competencies, intellectual development may be compromised. Foundational courses exist precisely to cultivate independent reasoning. When automation substitutes for formation, assessment becomes unreliable.

Second, authorship ambiguity. Without explicit disclosure practices and integration standards, academic integrity policies struggle to distinguish collaboration from substitution. Faculty cannot assess what remains invisible.

Third, inequitable development. Students who independently develop advanced prompting and evaluation skills may outperform peers who lack exposure or guidance. Inconsistent expectations across courses amplify disparities.

Fourth, assessment incoherence. When AI use is undefined, faculty struggle to determine what constitutes original intellectual contribution. Rubrics designed for singular authorship become inadequate in hybrid human-AI contexts.

These risks do not argue for prohibition. They argue for design.

Higher education has repeatedly demonstrated that structured integration mitigates technological disruption. When institutions articulate clear developmental pathways, students learn to engage new tools critically rather than passively. They develop discernment rather than dependency.

The Institutional Responsibility of Higher Education

Universities do more than transmit content. They cultivate intellectual habits, ethical reasoning, and disciplined inquiry. Artificial intelligence intersects with each of these responsibilities.

AI systems influence public discourse, civic participation, healthcare decisions, financial modeling, creative production, and theological reflection. Graduates must be equipped to use AI efficiently and to evaluate its social implications and epistemological limitations.

This moment requires clarity: AI integration is fundamentally a curricular design decision, whatever its technological trappings.

Institutions must determine when independent cognitive performance is essential, when AI can serve as a drafting or feedback partner, and when students must critically interrogate automated systems as objects of analysis.

The AI-Course Application Matrix (AI-CAM)

To meet this responsibility, institutions require a coherent framework that moves beyond binary permission structures. Artificial intelligence in academic settings cannot be reduced to "allowed" or "prohibited." It must be aligned with pedagogical purpose.

The AI-Course Application Matrix (AI-CAM) provides such alignment.

AI-CAM identifies seven levels of AI integration, ranging from complete restriction to fully AI-integrated course architecture across three dimensions: Access, Learning, and Architecture.

Dimension	Questions Addressed
Access	Is AI prohibited, permitted, encouraged, or required?
Learning	Is AI merely a tool, an object of critique, or an explicit competency?
Architecture	Is AI used in an assignment, throughout recurring work, or across the course environment?

The matrix does not impose uniformity. It provides coherence. The AI-CAM levels may be seen as common configurations across those dimensions.

Each level corresponds not merely to tool access but to a pedagogical stance regarding authorship, skill development, ethical responsibility, and assessment design. Faculty may designate different assignments with a course at different levels based on developmental stage, disciplinary norms, and institutional values, and different levels for entire courses.

At lower levels, AI may be restricted to preserve foundational cognitive development. At middle levels, AI use may be permitted or required within structured evaluative assignments. At advanced levels, AI literacy becomes embedded in learning outcomes, and AI tools are architecturally integrated into feedback and instructional systems—while faculty retain evaluative authority.

The movement across levels mirrors student development. Early stages emphasize independence and transparency. Intermediate stages cultivate evaluative reasoning. Advanced stages require disciplined collaboration and system-level awareness.

AI-Course Application Matrix (AI-CAM)

Level	Type of Integration	Description	Comments
0	AI Restricted or Prohibited	AI tools are not permitted unless explicitly authorized by the instructor. Used to benchmark independent cognitive performance or preserve foundational skill development.	Pros: Preserves authorship clarity; protects foundational skills; simplifies integrity enforcement. Cons: Artificial separation from contemporary tools; limits AI literacy development; enforcement challenges.
1	AI Permitted with Citation	Students may use AI tools but must formally cite their use in accordance with approved academic standards.	Pros: Promotes transparency and ethical awareness; minimal disruption to the curriculum. Cons: Limited instructional transformation; AI literacy remains incidental.
2	AI Encouraged	AI may be used for brainstorming,	Pros: Reduces student anxiety; supports

	for Support Tasks	outlining, generating feedback, providing study support, and revision, with citations required.	drafting and revision; introduces responsible usage. Cons: Uneven prompting skills; potential shallow engagement; boundary clarity required.
3	AI-Required Assignment(s)	One or more assignments require structured AI use, including critical evaluation and reflective analysis of outputs.	Pros: Develops critical AI evaluation, measurable literacy, and strengthens comparative reasoning. Cons: Increased faculty design time; risk of tool-focus over disciplinary depth.
4	AI Literacy Embedded in Learning Outcomes	Course learning outcomes explicitly include measurable AI literacy competencies integrated with disciplinary objectives.	Pros: Aligns with workforce demands; supports metacognition; enables coherent assessment. Cons: Requires curricular revision; faculty development is necessary; possible accreditation implications.
5	Structured AI Collaboration	Multiple recurring activities integrate AI as an intellectual partner in analysis, simulation, drafting, and iterative revision.	Pros: Deep iterative learning; scalable feedback; enhanced engagement. Cons: Blurred authorship boundaries; rubric refinement required; initial workload increase.

6	AI-Integrated Course Architecture	AI is embedded within instructional design, feedback systems, and assessment scaffolds, while faculty retain evaluative authority and serve as mentors and academic guarantors.	Pros: Personalized pathways; scalable formative feedback; system-level innovation. Cons: Technological dependence; governance concerns; data management complexity.

developed by Dr. Rick Upchurch

The architectural language used throughout this book is intentional. AI-CAM is not simply a framework for integrating artificial intelligence into individual courses. It represents a way of thinking about curriculum, faculty work, and institutional design that ultimately points beyond course development toward what will later be described as **the Architectural University**: an institution in which educational decisions are guided by coherent developmental purpose rather than by technological reaction. The chapters that follow build progressively toward that larger vision.

From Exposure to Formation

Exposure to AI does not produce literacy. Formation does.

Students already encounter AI outside the classroom. The institutional task is to focus on or direct the use of AI to achieve student learning. Structured integration ensures that students learn to question AI-generated content, verify claims, recognize bias, and articulate their intellectual contribution. They practice maintaining authorship even when using AI to assist them.

Properly designed AI integration accomplishes two simultaneous aims. It safeguards academic integrity and strengthens intellectual formation. Rather than displacing human reasoning, structured integration amplifies critical thinking, reflection, and metacognition.

Intentional design will determine whether artificial intelligence becomes a shortcut, or a catalyst for disciplined, ethical, and intellectually rigorous learning.

Chapter 2: The AI-CAM as Blueprint — Operationalizing C.L.E.A.R. Across All Levels of Integration

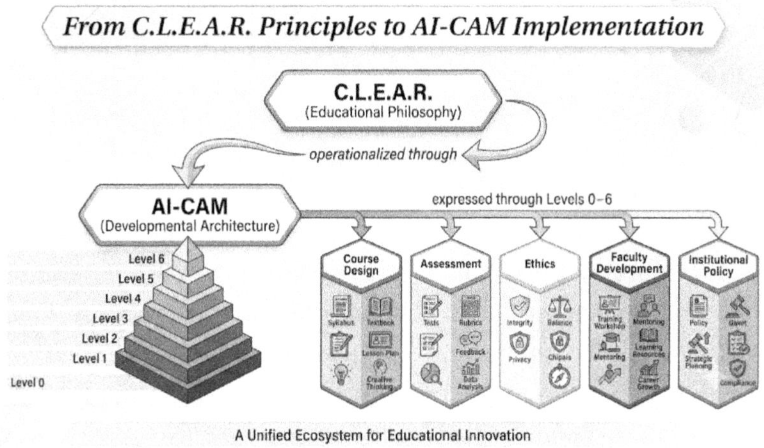

A paradigm for AI integration must do more than articulate values; it must translate those values into structured implementation. The AI-Course Application Matrix (AI-CAM) provides the structural blueprint for institutional and course-level decision-making. While C.L.E.A.R. defines the governing principles of responsible integration—Critical Thinking, Learning Outcomes, Ethical Use, Alignment, and Reflection—the AI-CAM operationalizes those principles across seven progressive levels of adoption.

In this model, C.L.E.A.R. supplies the evaluative lens; AI-CAM supplies the architectural design. Together, they form a coherent system for scalable, ethical, and pedagogically sound AI integration.

The Relationship Between C.L.E.A.R. and AI-CAM

The **C.L.E.A.R. Framework** articulates the educational philosophy that should govern the responsible integration of AI. It identifies five enduring principles that should characterize any AI-enabled learning environment:

- Critical Thinking
- Learning Outcomes
- Ethical Use
- Alignment
- Reflection

These principles remain constant regardless of discipline, institutional type, or future changes in AI technology.

The **AI-Course Application Matrix (AI-CAM)** is the operational model that implements those principles within actual courses. Rather than asking faculty merely to endorse the values represented by C.L.E.A.R., AI-CAM provides a structured developmental pathway that makes those values visible in course design, assessment, and institutional practice.

In short, C.L.E.A.R. establishes the philosophical commitments, while AI-CAM provides the structural architecture through which those commitments are enacted. At the course level, that architecture shapes instructional design, assessment, and student development. At the institutional level, the same principles point toward a broader educational vision, which this book will later describe as the Architectural University.

AI-CAM provides the curricular architecture through which those commitments are enacted.

Every AI-CAM level, from Level 0 through Level 6, should therefore be understood as a different developmental expression of the same C.L.E.A.R. principles rather than a different educational philosophy.

Faculty use C.L.E.A.R. to evaluate whether their design is educationally sound, and they use AI-CAM to determine how those principles should be implemented at an appropriate stage of learner development.

C — Critical Thinking Within the AI-CAM Structure

Critical thinking is not automatically produced by exposure to AI. It must be intentionally designed at each level of integration.

At Level 0 (AI Restricted), critical thinking is cultivated through independent cognitive performance. Students demonstrate unaided reasoning to establish baseline competence. Here, AI-CAM protects foundational intellectual development.

At Level 1 (AI Permitted with Citation), critical thinking grounds itself in transparency. By requiring students to articulate an AI system's contribution, citation catalyzes metacognitive awareness: students must evaluate what the tool generated, what they modified, and why.

At Level 2 (AI Encouraged for Support Tasks), critical thinking deepens through comparison and refinement. Students use AI for brainstorming or feedback but retain responsibility for synthesis. Faculty design prompts that require students to evaluate AI suggestions rather than merely accept them.

At Level 3 (AI-Required Assignment), structured evaluation becomes explicit. Students critique AI outputs, identify bias, test accuracy, and compare AI reasoning with disciplinary standards. Critical thinking becomes measurable.

At Level 4 (AI Literacy Embedded in Outcomes), evaluation of AI systems becomes a competency. Students analyze the model's limitations, the data sources, and the epistemological assumptions.

At Level 5 (Structured AI Collaboration), critical thinking becomes iterative and dialogical. Students engage AI as an intellectual partner while continuously exercising discernment and disciplinary judgment.

At Level 6 (AI-Integrated Course Architecture), critical thinking extends to systems awareness. Students learn not only to critique outputs but to understand how AI structures influence knowledge formation itself.

Across the matrix, critical thinking evolves from independence to discernment to systems-level evaluation.

L — Learning Outcomes and Competency Design Across Levels

C.L.E.A.R. requires that AI integration be tied to measurable outcomes. The AI-CAM ensures this alignment progresses intentionally.

At Levels 0–2, learning outcomes remain primarily disciplinary, with AI functioning as either restricted or supportive. AI literacy is introduced but not yet central.

At Level 3, AI competency becomes assessable. Assignments include explicit criteria such as "evaluate AI-generated claims using disciplinary standards."

At Level 4, AI literacy is embedded directly into course learning outcomes. "AI literacy should be cultivated as a transversal, institution-wide competence." (Medina-Gual et al. 2025, p.15) For example:

- Students will demonstrate the ability to assess AI-generated analyses for methodological bias.
- Students will integrate AI tools ethically to enhance domain-specific problem-solving.

At Levels 5 and 6, outcomes reflect collaborative and architectural integration. Students demonstrate iterative refinement using AI tools, interpret AI-assisted simulations, and apply AI-supported analytics responsibly.

The AI-CAM thus prevents superficial adoption. Each level requires clarity about what students should know, do, and demonstrate regarding AI.

E — Ethical Use as a Developmental Competency

Ethical use should not be perceived as a static policy statement. Appropriate ethical use is a developmental progression embedded across the AI-CAM levels.

At Level 0, ethics focuses on authorship integrity and the preservation of skill.

At Level 1, formal citation practices introduce transparency. Students disclose their tool usage in accordance with institutional standards.

At Level 2, ethical boundaries expand to include appropriate versus inappropriate use. Faculty clarify where AI assistance ends, and student authorship begins.

At Level 3, students critically examine bias, misinformation, intellectual property implications, and data limitations within AI outputs.

At Level 4, ethical reasoning becomes embedded in measurable outcomes. Students analyze algorithmic bias, societal implications, and responsible deployment within their discipline.

At Level 5, ethical collaboration is emphasized. Students must articulate their intellectual contribution in AI-assisted work, preserving human agency.

At Level 6, governance and data stewardship emerge. Ethical reflection includes privacy concerns, system dependence, and institutional accountability.

The AI-CAM ensures ethical formation matures alongside technological integration.

A — Alignment with Pedagogy, Assessment, and Institutional Standards

Alignment prevents AI from becoming disruptive or ornamental.

At early levels, alignment means containment. AI is either restricted or permitted in ways that protect course integrity.

At mid-levels (3–4), alignment requires redesign. Assignments, rubrics, and grading criteria explicitly account for AI involvement. Faculty refine evaluation methods to distinguish critical engagement from passive acceptance.

At advanced levels (5–6), alignment becomes architectural. AI tools are embedded in feedback systems, formative assessments, and scaffolding structures. Faculty retain evaluative authority, but AI assists in personalization and iteration.

Institutionally, AI-CAM enables programmatic coherence. Courses at different levels can coexist strategically. Foundational courses may remain at Level 0 or 1, yet have assignments at a higher level, while capstone experiences may operate at Levels 4–6, but still contain assignments at a lower level.

Alignment ensures AI enhances rather than distorts pedagogical intention.

R — Reflection and Continuous Improvement

Reflection transforms AI integration from implementation to innovation.

At Level 1, reflection may involve brief disclosures about AI use.

At Level 2, students reflect on how AI influenced their drafting process.

At Level 3, structured reflection evaluates the strengths and weaknesses of AI outputs.

At Level 4, metacognitive awareness becomes formalized: students articulate how AI shapes knowledge construction in their discipline.

At Levels 5 and 6, reflection expands to course and system design. Faculty analyze assessment data, evaluate AI tool effectiveness, and revise integration strategies.

The AI-CAM supports iterative advancement. A course may begin at Level 2 and progress as faculty capacity and institutional readiness grow.

C.L.E.A.R. and AI-CAM: Philosophy and Architecture

C.L.E.A.R. provides the normative philosophy that defines responsible AI integration. AI-CAM provides the developmental architecture through which those principles are implemented in curriculum design. They are not competing frameworks but complementary components of a single educational model.

Their complementary relationship also explains why AI-CAM should not be viewed merely as a course-design framework. Course design is its immediate application, but institutional architecture is its larger aspiration. As faculty, departments, and academic leaders begin making educational decisions from a shared developmental philosophy, they move incrementally toward an institution whose coherence arises from educational purpose rather than technological circumstance. That emerging vision provides the foundation for the concept of **the Architectural University**, developed in the concluding chapter of this book.

The result is more than responsible AI adoption. It is the gradual development of an educational philosophy in which technology consistently serves human learning rather than defining it. AI-CAM provides the developmental architecture through which that philosophy becomes visible in courses, curricula, and, eventually, in institutions themselves.

Chapter 3: Ethical Foundations of AI in Course Design: An AI-CAM Perspective

Artificial intelligence does not become ethical simply by being permitted. Ethical use must be intentionally designed, scaffolded, and assessed. The AI-CAM operationalizes the ethical commitments established in the C.L.E.A.R. framework by translating ethical principles into concrete decisions about course design. Every decision about whether, when, and how students may use AI carries implications for authorship, responsibility, transparency, intellectual formation, privacy, and equity.

The ethical dimensions of AI, however, should not be understood as belonging to particular AI-CAM levels. Academic integrity is not simply a Level 0 concern, just as transparency does not begin at Level 1 and privacy does not suddenly emerge at the higher levels of integration. These responsibilities extend across the entire AI-CAM continuum. What changes as AI integration increases is the nature and complexity of the ethical decisions faculty, students, and institutions must make.

AI-CAM describes increasing levels of AI integration, not increasing levels of ethical maturity. Level 6 is not inherently more ethical than Level 0. In some circumstances, prohibiting AI may be the most responsible educational choice; in others, integrating AI more deeply may better prepare students for the intellectual and professional environments they will encounter. Ethical course design requires faculty to select the level of integration that serves the educational purpose while addressing the responsibilities that accompany that choice.

Six ethical concerns:

1. *Academic Integrity Beyond Plagiarism Detection*

Much of the early conversation about generative AI in higher education focused on cheating. The concern was understandable. Students suddenly had access to tools capable of producing essays, solving problems, summarizing readings, generating computer code, and completing many of the tasks traditionally used as evidence of student learning.

Yet defining academic integrity primarily in terms of whether a student personally produced every word of an assignment is increasingly inadequate. AI-CAM requires a broader conception of integrity centered on cognitive authenticity.

Cognitive authenticity asks whether student work provides legitimate evidence of the knowledge, reasoning, judgment, or skill that an assignment is intended to develop or measure. The fundamental question is therefore not simply, *Did the student use AI?* It is, *Does the completed work authentically demonstrate the learning the assignment was designed to represent?*

The difference between disclosure and cognitive authenticity matters because AI use can compromise the latter even when it has been properly acknowledged. A student might properly cite an AI system that generated an analysis while still bypassing the reasoning that the assignment was intended to develop. Conversely, a student might use AI extensively in an assignment specifically designed to teach critical evaluation, iterative problem solving, or human-AI collaboration without compromising academic integrity at all.

The ethical responsibility of the faculty member is therefore to determine what intellectual work must remain with the student.

At Level 0, protecting cognitive authenticity may require independent performance. A first-year writing instructor, for example, might require students to complete an initial essay without AI assistance to obtain an accurate picture of each student's writing ability. The restriction is not based on distrust of students or hostility toward technology. It serves a legitimate educational purpose: establishing what the student can independently do.

At higher levels, cognitive authenticity takes different forms. When AI is permitted or encouraged, assignments must make clear which aspects of the intellectual process may be assisted and which remain the student's responsibility. This understanding of cognitive authenticity parallels Wiggins's (1990) distinction between directly examining performance on worthy intellectual tasks and relying on simplified proxies to infer competence.

When AI is required, students may need to evaluate, correct, challenge, or improve AI-generated material. In highly integrated courses, assessment design must distinguish between the productive use of AI and the disciplinary judgment students themselves are expected to demonstrate.

Academic integrity, therefore, becomes more than plagiarism detection or enforcement. It becomes a question of assessment validity and intellectual responsibility. Faculty must be able to answer a fundamental question: What evidence of student learning does this assignment provide when AI is available?

2. Transparency, Attribution, and Intellectual Responsibility

Ethical AI use also requires transparency. Students, faculty, and evaluators should be able to understand when AI has contributed meaningfully to academic work and what role it played.

At lower levels of AI integration, this may be accomplished through relatively simple citation or disclosure requirements. A student who uses AI to brainstorm ideas, revise prose, or generate feedback might identify the tool used and describe the nature of the assistance received. Such practices reinforce the principle that intellectual assistance should not be hidden.

Citation alone, however, does not fully resolve the ethical issue.

Consequently, students may need to explain not only *that* AI was used but also *how* it influenced the intellectual process.

Consider a business communication course in which students are permitted to use AI to improve grammar and tone. A disclosure statement that identifies the tool and explains its purpose may be sufficient. In an engineering design course where AI contributes to modeling decisions, however, greater transparency is necessary. Students may need to document AI-assisted decisions, explain which recommendations they accepted or rejected, and describe how results were independently validated.

As integration increases across AI-CAM, transparency shifts from procedural disclosure to intellectual accountability. Students should increasingly be able to explain the relationship between AI assistance and their own judgment.

The ethical goal is the development of intellectual responsibility. Students should learn that using AI does not transfer responsibility for the resulting work to the machine. The student remains responsible for what is submitted, claimed, recommended, or concluded.

3. Bias, Hallucination, and Epistemic Reliability

Generative AI poses a particularly important challenge for higher education because it can produce information that appears authoritative without possessing scholarly authority. AI-generated responses may be accurate, partially accurate, misleading, biased, or entirely fabricated, yet presented with similar confidence and fluency.

Higher education has always required students to distinguish between assertion and evidence, evaluate sources, recognize competing interpretations, and justify conclusions. Generative AI makes those habits more important because linguistic fluency can easily be mistaken for epistemic reliability. A polished answer may appear credible even when its factual or interpretive foundation is weak.

Faculty, therefore, have an ethical responsibility to teach students that AI output is *not* equivalent to scholarly evidence. Verification cannot be treated as an optional step added after generation. It must become part of responsible AI use.

For example, students in a history course might ask an AI system to interpret a significant historical event and then compare its account with primary sources and peer-reviewed scholarship. The educational purpose is not merely to catch the AI when it makes mistakes. Students examine what the system emphasizes, what it omits, what assumptions appear within its interpretation, and why scholarly authority cannot be delegated to an automated system.

At more advanced levels, students should also consider systemic limitations. Training data may reproduce historical biases, dominant cultural assumptions, or uneven representation. Different systems may generate different answers to the same question. Responsible AI literacy, therefore, requires students to evaluate not only individual outputs but also the conditions under which those outputs are produced.

These concerns extend beyond the accuracy of individual outputs. Yan et al. (2024), in a systematic review of 118 studies, identified transparency, privacy, equality, and beneficence as recurring ethical challenges in educational applications of large language models. Blodgett et al. (2020) further caution that claims about technological bias should identify the groups affected, the harms produced, and the normative standards by which those harms are judged.

The ethical objective is disciplined epistemic judgment: knowing when AI can assist inquiry while recognizing that responsibility for determining what is credible remains human.

4. Data Privacy and Student Data Governance

AI integration creates responsibilities regarding the information students and faculty provide to external systems. Prompts may contain personal information, student work, research data, institutional information, or other material that should not be casually transferred to an AI platform. Once information enters such a system, users may have limited knowledge of how it is stored, processed, retained, or subsequently used.

At lower levels of AI-CAM integration, responsible practice may be relatively straightforward. Faculty can discourage students from entering sensitive information and avoid assignments that unnecessarily require personal data. Students should understand that convenience does not eliminate responsibility for their digital footprint.

As AI becomes more deeply embedded in learning activities, however, the privacy questions become more consequential. The ethical principle remains consistent across the continuum: educational benefit does not eliminate the obligation to protect student information.

The deeper the integration, the more important it becomes to recognize that privacy is not simply a technical issue. It is a matter of educational stewardship and respect for students as persons.

5. Equity Implications and the Digital Divide

AI can expand educational opportunity, but it can also reproduce or deepen existing inequalities. Access to devices, reliable internet connections, advanced AI systems, technical knowledge, and effective prompting skills is not uniformly distributed among students.

For this reason, ethical AI integration cannot assume that allowing students to use AI creates equal opportunity to benefit from it.

At lower levels of integration, equity may require relatively modest interventions. If the use of AI is permitted or encouraged, faculty should ensure that students unfamiliar with the technology are not placed at an immediate disadvantage. A literature instructor who encourages AI-supported brainstorming, for example, might provide introductory instruction, sample prompts, and opportunities for guided practice before expecting students to use AI independently.

The issue becomes more significant when the use of AI is required. Once the successful completion of an assignment depends upon access to AI, equitable access becomes an instructional responsibility rather than a student convenience.

At higher levels, where AI literacy may become an explicit learning outcome or AI may be integrated throughout the course, students need reasonable opportunities to develop the competencies being assessed. A nursing program that incorporates AI-assisted diagnostic simulations, for example, cannot reasonably assume that all students will independently arrive with equivalent technological experience. Instruction in the responsible use of those systems becomes part of the educational task.

There is also a less visible dimension of equity. Students enter courses with different levels of confidence, technological experience, disciplinary preparation, and familiarity with AI. Faculty must ensure that AI integration does not inadvertently reward prior technological privilege rather than the learning the course is intended to foster.

Equity becomes more consequential as AI becomes more central to learning. The ethical principle is straightforward: students should not be educationally disadvantaged because an institution or instructor has chosen to incorporate AI into the learning environment.

6. Institutional Policy Alignment

Some ethical responsibilities created by AI can be addressed within the individual classroom. Others cannot.

A faculty member can establish appropriate boundaries for an assignment, require transparency, teach students to verify AI-generated information, and design assessments that preserve cognitive authenticity. But individual faculty members cannot independently determine institutional data protections, guarantee equitable access to approved technologies, reconcile conflicting academic policies, or establish university-wide standards for accountability.

At lower levels of AI-CAM, many ethical decisions remain primarily instructional. Faculty determine when AI may be used, what forms of assistance are appropriate, and how students should disclose that assistance. As AI becomes more deeply integrated into courses and programs, those decisions increasingly intersect with responsibilities shared across the institution.

This does not mean that institutions should impose a single model of AI use across all courses. Such uniformity would contradict the developmental logic of AI-CAM. A foundational assignment may appropriately require independent performance, while an advanced professional course may require substantial AI collaboration. Even within a single course, different assignments may appropriately operate at different levels.

Institutional responsibility, therefore, should not be confused with instructional uniformity. The ethical goal is coherence: students and faculty should operate within an environment in which expectations are understandable, responsibilities are identifiable, and institutional practices do not undermine legitimate educational decisions.

This is one reason a shared framework such as AI-CAM matters beyond the individual classroom. It provides a language through which faculty, programs, and institutions can discuss different forms of AI integration without assuming that a single approach is appropriate everywhere.

The mechanisms through which institutions create that coherence are addressed directly in Chapter 14. The ethical foundation comes first: as institutions integrate AI into the educational environment, they assume responsibility for the conditions under which that integration occurs.

Conclusion: From Compliance to Responsibility

Ethical AI integration cannot be reduced to a question of whether students are permitted to use a particular technology. Nor can it be achieved simply by adding an AI statement to a syllabus. Ethical course design requires faculty to consider what students are being asked to learn, what intellectual responsibilities must remain theirs, what forms of assistance should be visible, how knowledge claims will be evaluated, what information should be protected, and whether students have a meaningful opportunity to participate in the learning environment being created.

The AI-CAM helps faculty make those decisions intentionally. Its levels describe different relationships between AI and learning, but every level carries ethical responsibilities. Restriction requires justification. Permission requires clarity. Required use requires purposeful design. Embedded AI literacy requires meaningful assessment. Structured collaboration requires careful attention to authorship and judgment. Architectural integration extends responsibility beyond the individual classroom.

As AI integration deepens, responsibility increasingly extends beyond the choices of individual students and faculty. Questions of privacy, access, accountability, and appropriate use eventually require both institutional and instructional responses. Those broader responsibilities become increasingly important as the discussion moves from course design to institutional architecture later in this book.

Ethical AI integration occurs when academic integrity, transparency, epistemic judgment, privacy, equity, and accountability are not treated as restrictions on AI use but as design principles that shape the educational environment itself.

Chapter 4: Outcomes Assessment in AI-Integrated Courses: An AI-CAM Framework

Assessment in AI-integrated courses cannot remain static while instructional design evolves. When artificial intelligence becomes part of the learning environment, it also affects what must be assessed, how it is assessed, and why it is assessed. Because C.L.E.A.R. requires alignment between learning, assessment, ethics, and reflection, AI-CAM provides the developmental structure through which that alignment is assessed across Levels 0–6.

Assessment in AI-integrated environments must address five interlocking dimensions: disciplinary mastery, AI literacy, ethical application, cognitive authenticity, and institutional accountability. As courses move through AI-CAM Levels 0–6, assessment practices must develop accordingly. The central question is not whether AI is present, but whether the assessment strategy remains constructively aligned with course outcomes and the designated level of AI integration.

Constructive Alignment Across AI-CAM Levels

Constructive alignment requires that learning outcomes, learning activities, and assessments reinforce one another. In AI-integrated courses, this alignment must explicitly reflect the designated AI-CAM level.

At Level 0 (AI Restricted or Prohibited), assessment focuses exclusively on independent cognitive performance. Exams, in-class writing, oral defenses, and proctored demonstrations establish baseline competence. The assessment question is clear: Can the student perform foundational tasks without AI assistance?

At Levels 1–2 (AI Permitted or Encouraged for Support Tasks), assessments must differentiate between acceptable assistance and intellectual substitution. Rubrics should measure both the quality of disciplinary content and the appropriateness and transparency of AI use. Disclosure statements, revision logs, and reflective annotations become part of the evaluative process.

At Levels 3–4 (AI-Required Assignments; AI Literacy Embedded in Outcomes), assessments must explicitly measure AI literacy competencies alongside disciplinary knowledge. Students are not merely permitted to use AI; they are evaluated on how critically and responsibly they use it.

At Levels 5–6 (Structured Collaboration; AI-Integrated Architecture), assessment expands to include process analytics, iterative refinement, and system-level documentation. Faculty assesses judgment, decision-making, validation practices, and professional reasoning within AI-mediated environments.

Without level-specific alignment, assessment becomes incoherent. With alignment, AI integration becomes measurable and defensible.

Measuring Disciplinary Mastery and AI Literacy

A persistent concern in AI-enabled environments is that generative outputs can mask gaps in subject-matter mastery. The solution lies not in defensive prohibition, but in differentiated assessment strategies.

Disciplinary mastery measures content knowledge, conceptual understanding, analytical reasoning, and applied competence within the field. AI literacy measures the student's ability to prompt effectively, evaluate outputs, detect bias, verify information, justify tool selection, and document usage responsibly. These two domains intersect but are not identical.

For example, in a Level 3 political science course, students might be required to use AI to generate policy summaries and then critique them. Assessment would include:

- Accuracy and depth of policy analysis (disciplinary mastery).
- Identification of AI limitations or distortions (AI literacy).
- Quality of verification against scholarly sources (critical reasoning).
- Transparency of documentation (ethical application).

Separating these dimensions within rubrics prevents AI fluency from compensating for weak disciplinary understanding. It also ensures that strong disciplinary students are not penalized for measured and appropriate AI restraint.

Designing Rubrics for Hybrid Authorship

Traditional rubrics are predicated on singular human authorship. AI-integrated environments, by contrast, demand frameworks optimized for hybrid authorship—the dynamic frontier where human reasoning intersects with machine assistance.

Rubrics should include distinct criteria such as:

- Intellectual Contribution: Evidence of original analysis, synthesis, or interpretation beyond AI-generated content.
- Critical Evaluation of AI Output: Demonstrated ability to assess accuracy, bias, and coherence.
- Integration Quality: Skill in revising, restructuring, or refining AI-generated material.
- Transparency and Documentation: Clear disclosure of AI usage and rationale.
- Ethical Compliance: Adherence to course and institutional AI policies.

For example, in a Level 4 engineering course where AI literacy is embedded in learning outcomes, a design project rubric might allocate separate scoring categories for technical feasibility, AI-assisted modeling documentation, validation testing, and reflective justification of tool use.

Such rubric structures reinforce that AI does not replace authorship; it reshapes it. Students are evaluated not merely for producing text or models, but for exercising informed judgment.

Assessing Process Alongside Product

AI integration can make invisible processes more visible when instructors intentionally design for it. Process documentation is especially critical at Levels 3–6.

Assessment of process may include:

- Prompt logs showing iterative refinement.
- Comparative analysis between AI drafts and final submissions.
- Reflection essays explaining decision-making.
- Version histories demonstrating substantive revision.
- Validation reports identifying fact-checking procedures.

In a Level 5 business analytics course that uses structured AI collaboration, students might submit a prompt-iteration portfolio documenting how successive refinements improved model performance. Assessment would consider not only the final output but also the sophistication of the iteration strategy and recognition of AI limitations.

This approach shifts emphasis from static products to intellectual formation. It measures habits of inquiry, skepticism, and disciplined reasoning.

Validity and Reliability in AI-Mediated Assessment

The integration of AI introduces new concerns about validity and reliability.

Validity requires that assessments measure intended learning outcomes rather than tool proficiency alone. A literature exam should still measure interpretive reasoning, not prompt-engineering skills, unless AI literacy is an explicit outcome. When AI is introduced into the instructional loop, tasks must be engineered so that successful performance hinges on higher-order synthesis rather than raw generative output.

Reliability requires consistency across evaluators and sections. Clear AI disclosure requirements, standardized rubric criteria, and explicit level designations reduce ambiguity. Institutional adoption of AI-CAM-level labeling across syllabi can improve consistency and reduce student confusion.

Faculty should also remain alert to algorithmic variability. When AI tools produce inconsistent outputs, assignments should require verification and cross-checking to prevent assessment from being influenced by model randomness rather than student judgment.

Documentation and Accreditation Considerations

Accrediting bodies increasingly expect institutions to demonstrate coherent assessment practices, academic integrity safeguards, and evidence of learning outcomes. AI integration heightens scrutiny in all three areas.

Documentation should include:

- Clear designation of AI-CAM level in syllabi.
- Alignment maps showing how AI literacy outcomes correspond to program objectives.
- Rubrics reflecting hybrid authorship criteria.
- Samples of AI disclosure statements.
- Evidence of faculty training and governance oversight.

At Level 6, where AI becomes embedded in the course architecture, institutions must also document data governance practices, algorithmic auditing procedures, and faculty retention of evaluative authority.

Such documentation demonstrates that AI integration is pedagogically intentional rather than technologically opportunistic.

A Developmental Model of Assessment Across AI-CAM

Assessment maturity parallels integration maturity.

Level 0 protects baseline competence.

Levels 1–2 cultivate transparency and responsible use of support.

Levels 3–4 measure critical AI literacy alongside disciplinary reasoning.

Levels 5–6 assess professional judgment within AI-mediated systems.

When assessment evolves in step with integration, AI does not erode academic standards. Instead, it expands what can be measured: critical evaluation of automated systems, ethical reasoning in digital contexts, and reflective judgment in collaborative human-machine environments.

Effective outcomes assessment in AI-integrated courses requires more than adapting old rubrics. It demands a rearticulation of what counts as evidence of learning. AI-CAM provides structural clarity to make that rearticulation coherent, progressive, and institutionally defensible.

Part II. Designing Developmentally Appropriate AI Integration

Introduction: How to Read the AI-CAM Levels

The seven levels of the AI-Course Application Matrix are easily misunderstood.

Presented in sequence from Level 0 through Level 6, they can appear to describe a progression toward increasingly sophisticated use of artificial intelligence, inviting the assumption that the objective of curriculum design is to move steadily upward until AI becomes fully integrated into every aspect of instruction. Such a reading is understandable. It is also inconsistent with the framework's purpose.

The faculty's responsibility has never been to maximize the use of educational technologies. It has been to determine which instructional approaches best serve students' intellectual development. Artificial intelligence changes neither that responsibility nor the principles by which it should be exercised. What it changes is the range of instructional decisions available to faculty.

The organizing question of AI-CAM is therefore not *How much AI should this course use?* It is *What role, if any, should AI play at this particular stage of student development?*

Every curriculum is developmental. Introductory courses establish foundational competencies upon which later learning depends. Intermediate courses cultivate analytical habits and disciplinary judgment. Advanced courses increasingly resemble professional practice, asking students to integrate knowledge, exercise independent judgment, and solve complex problems under authentic conditions. Good curriculum design has always recognized that students require different kinds of instruction at different stages of learning. Artificial intelligence should be integrated according to that same developmental logic.

This means that the AI-CAM levels should never be understood as rankings.

A Level 5 course is not inherently better than a Level 2 course, just as a doctoral seminar is not inherently better than an introductory composition course. Each serves a different educational purpose because it serves learners at different stages of development. The appropriate AI-CAM level is therefore determined not by the technology's sophistication but by the learner's developmental needs and the course's educational purpose.

Indeed, one of the most common institutional mistakes is assuming that greater AI integration necessarily represents educational progress. Across institutions, I have found the opposite to be true. Courses become stronger not when they incorporate more artificial intelligence, but when they incorporate it more intentionally. In some settings, that intentionality requires substantial AI integration. In others, it requires very little. There are moments in every curriculum when independent cognitive performance remains the most pedagogically appropriate design. There are equally compelling moments when students should learn to evaluate, supervise, and collaborate with AI. Educational wisdom lies in recognizing the difference.

For that reason, each chapter in this section addresses three questions.

The first is pedagogical. What educational logic makes this level the appropriate choice? Rather than presenting each level as a collection of permissions and restrictions, the chapters explain the underlying curriculum principle that gives the level coherence. Every level exists because it solves a particular instructional problem. Understanding that problem is more important than memorizing the policy.

The second question is practical. What does successful implementation actually look like? Here the emphasis shifts from theory to design. Assignment construction, assessment practices, and expectations for transparency are considered together as components of a coherent instructional strategy. The goal is not to provide recipes that can be copied uncritically, but to illustrate what alignment looks like when course design, assessment, and AI expectations reinforce one another.

The third question is cautionary. How does this level typically fail? Every level has characteristic weaknesses when its pedagogical purpose is misunderstood. These failures are rarely the result of faculty indifference or technological incompetence. More often they emerge when AI policies become disconnected from learning objectives, when implementation drifts away from its original educational purpose, or when institutions mistake technological capability for pedagogical necessity. Understanding these recurring patterns allows faculty to avoid them before they become embedded in course design.

Together, these three questions reflect the central conviction of this book: *artificial intelligence belongs in a curriculum only when it advances learning appropriate to a student's developmental stage.*

Seen from this perspective, the movement from Level 0 to Level 5 is less a journey toward greater technological sophistication than a progression in the relationship between learner, discipline, and technology. Early levels protect the development of independent cognition and intellectual accountability. Middle levels teach students to use AI responsibly while strengthening disciplinary judgment. Advanced levels prepare students to exercise professional authority within increasingly AI-mediated environments without surrendering the evaluative responsibility that remains uniquely human.

That developmental progression is the architecture of AI-CAM.

It also explains why the framework should remain durable even as individual AI systems continue to evolve. The technologies will change. Their capabilities will expand. New platforms will replace old ones. Yet the developmental questions confronting faculty will remain remarkably consistent. Students will still need foundational knowledge before advanced application. They will still need to distinguish reliable information from unreliable information. They will still need to develop professional judgment before supervising increasingly capable technologies. Those educational realities are far more stable than any particular software platform.

Ultimately, the purpose of AI-CAM is to encourage more thoughtful teaching, not simply more AI or less AI.

Artificial intelligence becomes educationally valuable only when it serves the larger work of intellectual formation. That work has always been developmental. It remains developmental today. The chapters that follow examine what that developmental progression looks like in practice, one level at a time.

Chapter 5: Preserving Foundational Learning - Level 0 - AI Restricted or Prohibited

Developmental Principle: *Foundational competencies should be developed independently before being augmented by technology.*

Why Choose This Level?

The educational question is not whether AI is present. It already is. The question is whether its use is appropriate to the developmental task students are undertaking at a particular moment in their learning.

Every level within the framework begins with the learner rather than the technology. Before asking what artificial intelligence can contribute to a course, faculty must first ask what intellectual formation the course is intended to accomplish. Only then can they determine whether AI advances that purpose, complicates it, or temporarily needs to be set aside.

Level 0 exists because every curriculum includes moments when independent cognitive performance is the learning objective.

Across disciplines, these moments take different forms. A first-year writing instructor may need to observe how students organize their ideas before offering revision instruction. A mathematics professor may need to know whether students genuinely understand algebraic reasoning before introducing computational tools. Nursing faculty may need to determine whether students can recognize clinical deterioration before decision-support systems are integrated into the instructional environment. A theology professor may ask students to wrestle directly with a primary text before consulting secondary interpretations. Although these examples differ considerably in content, they share a common educational purpose. *Faculty are attempting to observe what students can do before technological assistance begins to shape the learning process.*

This is the developmental logic of Level 0.

Independent performance is not preserved because artificial intelligence is inherently undesirable. It is preserved because certain forms of learning cannot be evaluated accurately once technological mediation becomes part of the process. The instructional value lies not simply in the final product but in the evidence that independent work reveals. Misconceptions and habits of reasoning become visible in ways that technology-assisted work can easily obscure.

Seen in this way, Level 0 functions less as a policy on artificial intelligence than as a diagnostic strategy within curriculum design.

Faculty have always created learning experiences that intentionally limit the resources available. Closed-book examinations, oral defenses, laboratory practicums, language immersion exercises, and supervised clinical demonstrations all operate according to the same principle. They isolate specific competencies so they can be observed with clarity. The temporary absence of certain tools is not intended to make learning more difficult. Rather, it allows faculty to determine whether the underlying intellectual structures have been established before additional supports are introduced.

Artificial intelligence should be understood within this same tradition.

When AI is restricted at Level 0, the restriction is instructional rather than punitive. Over the past several years, I have observed a remarkably consistent pattern during faculty development workshops. Instructors rarely begin the conversation by saying they want to prohibit AI because they oppose innovation. Much more often, they describe uncertainty about what they are actually assessing. They can no longer determine whether a student's essay reflects the student's own analytical abilities or the language model's organizational strengths. They question whether introductory programming assignments still reveal computational thinking or simply effective prompting. They worry that early clinical case analyses show greater familiarity with AI-generated recommendations than with independent diagnostic reasoning.

This observation points toward a broader principle that extends well beyond AI. Higher education has always assumed that learning is developmental. Foundational knowledge precedes application. Application precedes synthesis. Synthesis precedes professional judgment. Every curriculum embodies this progression, whether it is explicitly stated or not. Artificial intelligence does not eliminate developmental sequencing. If anything, it underscores the importance of recognizing it, because powerful technologies can make it appear competence has been achieved before it actually has.

The distinction between performance and development is therefore critical.

Students may produce increasingly sophisticated work with AI assistance while still lacking the conceptual understanding needed to evaluate it independently. The danger is not that artificial intelligence produces poor assignments. Quite the opposite. *The danger is that it can produce work that appears to demonstrate competencies students have not yet developed.* Surface performance becomes a poor indicator of underlying learning.

Faculty have encountered versions of this problem before. Calculators changed mathematics instruction without eliminating the need for number sense. Spell checkers improved written communication without replacing the need to understand language. Statistical software transformed research without removing the necessity of methodological reasoning. In each case, educators eventually distinguished between competencies that required independent mastery and competencies that could appropriately be augmented by technology.

Artificial intelligence invites precisely the same distinction.

Level 0, therefore, should not be understood as opposition to AI. Nor should it be viewed as the permanent state toward which every course ought to aspire. It represents a temporary instructional environment in which faculty intentionally preserve opportunities for students to construct foundational knowledge through their own intellectual effort before introducing technologies that can assist that work.

The emphasis on "before" is essential.

Developmental sequencing does not argue against AI integration. It argues for integrating AI at the appropriate point in the learning process.

The purpose of foundational instruction is to develop judgment, not simply to accumulate knowledge. Judgment emerges through repeated encounters with complexity, uncertainty, error, revision, and reflection. Those experiences are intellectually demanding precisely because they cannot be delegated to someone—or something—else. Artificial intelligence may eventually become an important partner in professional work, but partnership presupposes capacities that have already been formed.

Level 0 protects the formation of those capacities.

For that reason, the question faculty should ask is "What foundational competencies must students develop independently before AI becomes educationally beneficial?"

Once foundational competencies have been established, the educational question changes. Faculty no longer need to determine whether students can perform independently. They begin asking how artificial intelligence can be incorporated without obscuring authorship or intellectual responsibility.

That transition marks the movement to Level 1.

What Successful Implementation Looks Like

The success of Level 0 depends less on the existence of a restriction than on the clarity of its educational purpose. Students are remarkably perceptive. They can usually distinguish between a rule that exists because an instructor is uncomfortable with technology and one that exists because the instructor is intentionally designing a learning experience. The first often invites resistance. The second usually earns respect, even from students who would prefer fewer restrictions.

For that reason, successful Level 0 implementation begins with explanation rather than enforcement.

Faculty should tell students why independent performance matters in this course at this point in the curriculum. They should explain what competencies are being developed, why those competencies must first emerge without technological assistance, and how the course will eventually build upon them. Students need to understand that Level 0 is a judgment about the learner's developmental needs, not about artificial intelligence itself.

Successful Level 0 assignments focus on competencies that faculty genuinely need to observe independently. They are not designed simply because they are easy to monitor or enforce. Rather, they ask students to demonstrate forms of thinking that later instruction will assume as foundational.

A first-year composition course may require students to draft an analytical essay in class before introducing AI-assisted revision. A chemistry instructor may require students to solve problems independently before computational tools are used in laboratory work. A theology course may ask students to engage a biblical text through careful exegesis before consulting secondary commentaries or digital assistants. In each case, the assignment isolates a foundational intellectual activity whose development is essential to everything that follows.

One of the most common design mistakes is extending restriction to assignments where independent performance no longer serves a meaningful instructional purpose. Faculty sometimes continue prohibiting AI simply because it was prohibited earlier in the course. Yet developmental sequencing requires continual reassessment. Once students have demonstrated the competency Level 0 was intended to cultivate, instructional design should evolve accordingly. A restriction is justified only so long as it serves the developmental objective that gave rise to it.

The objective is not to eliminate every possibility of inappropriate AI use. No assessment system can accomplish that. The objective is to create enough opportunities for authentic intellectual performance that faculty can make informed instructional decisions about what students actually understand.

In many cases, the most valuable assessments at Level 0 are formative rather than summative.

Diagnostic essays reveal writing habits before grades carry significant consequences. Early programming exercises expose misconceptions that can be corrected before they become entrenched. Preliminary clinical simulations allow instructors to identify weaknesses in reasoning before students encounter more complex scenarios. Because Level 0 is fundamentally developmental, its greatest contribution often lies in informing subsequent instruction rather than assigning final evaluations.

Students should never experience Level 0 as a relationship of suspicion between instructor and learner. The atmosphere should instead communicate a shared commitment to intellectual formation. Faculty are not withholding technology because they distrust students. They are temporarily removing one form of assistance so that both instructor and student can see more clearly what has already been learned and what still requires attention.

When that culture exists, Level 0 often produces an unexpected benefit: students begin to recognize abilities they did not know they possessed.

One of the hidden dangers of premature AI integration is that students may begin attributing successful performance to the technology rather than to their own developing competence. Level 0 quietly reverses that tendency. Students experience firsthand that they can analyze, reason, write, calculate, interpret, and solve problems through their own intellectual effort. Artificial intelligence may later expand those capacities, but it does not create them.

Once learners possess confidence in their own emerging competence, artificial intelligence no longer threatens authorship. It becomes something different—a resource whose contributions can be acknowledged openly because students have already established a clear sense of where their own intellectual work begins.

Where This Level Fails

Every level of AI-CAM has characteristic failure modes. They are rarely the result of poor intentions. More often, they emerge because faculty, departments, or institutions misunderstand the developmental purpose for which the level was designed. Level 0 is no exception.

The most common misunderstanding is viewing restriction as the educational objective rather than as the instructional strategy. When this happens, faculty begin defending the absence of AI rather than asking what it is intended to accomplish. The conversation gradually shifts away from student development and toward technological prohibition. Artificial intelligence itself becomes the problem to be managed rather than one of many instructional variables to be considered within thoughtful curriculum design.

A Level 0 course should always be able to answer a simple question:

What developmental competency requires students to work independently at this point in the curriculum?

If that question cannot be answered clearly, the rationale for restriction has likely become detached from the educational purpose it was intended to serve.

A second failure emerges when faculty mistake independent performance for educational rigor.

There is a tendency in some academic conversations to assume that the more difficult an assignment becomes, the greater its educational value. Yet difficulty alone has never been the measure of effective teaching. Students can struggle productively, but they can also struggle unnecessarily. Level 0 is intended to maximize visibility, not difficulty. Faculty temporarily remove technological assistance to observe students' thinking more clearly, not because independent work is inherently superior to supported learning.

A well-designed Level 0 assignment should reveal the strengths and weaknesses that will guide subsequent instruction. If students complete independent work and the instructor simply assigns a grade before moving on, one of the principal educational advantages of Level 0 has been lost. Restriction without diagnostic response contributes little to learning. The independent work becomes valuable only when faculty use it to shape what follows.

Another institutional failure occurs when Level 0 becomes disconnected from the larger curriculum.

One recurring theme in this book is that AI-CAM is architectural rather than a collection of isolated course policies. Yet institutions sometimes implement Level 0 as though it existed independently of the other levels. Individual instructors prohibit AI without considering where students will encounter it later in the program. Departments maintain foundational restrictions but never intentionally transition toward responsible AI integration in more advanced coursework.

Students, therefore, experience a fragmented curriculum in which each course appears to operate on unrelated assumptions. This fragmentation creates confusion rather than development.

The educational purpose of Level 0 is not to produce graduates who have avoided AI. It is to produce graduates whose foundational competencies are sufficiently well developed that later AI integration strengthens rather than substitutes for their thinking. Restriction only makes sense when it forms part of a larger developmental sequence.

Perhaps the most significant failure, however, arises when institutions begin treating AI detection as the primary instructional strategy.

The emergence of increasingly sophisticated AI detection systems has understandably attracted considerable attention. Faculty want confidence that independent work is genuinely independent. Yet an overreliance on technological detection often reflects a misplaced educational emphasis. The conversation shifts from designing assignments that reveal authentic thinking to identifying assignments that are easier to police.

The architecture of a course should never be determined primarily by the ease with which misconduct can be detected. It should be determined by the developmental purposes for which the course exists.

Indeed, some of the strongest Level 0 courses require very little technological surveillance precisely because the instructional design itself makes independent thinking visible. Oral examinations, in-class writing, iterative drafting, laboratory demonstrations, design critiques, clinical observations, and supervised problem-solving all provide rich evidence of student understanding without requiring faculty to rely heavily on increasingly uncertain detection technologies.

Good pedagogy generally proves more durable than technological enforcement.

There is one final failure that deserves particular attention because it reflects a misunderstanding not simply of Level 0 but of the AI-CAM framework as a whole.

Some institutions begin treating Level 0 as the morally preferable level of AI integration. Others make precisely the opposite mistake, assuming that Level 0 represents educational backwardness and that every curriculum should move steadily toward Levels 5 and 6. Both assumptions misunderstand developmental sequencing.

The AI-CAM levels are not rankings. They are placements.

Each level answers a different educational question because students require different forms of instruction at different stages of learning. A foundational mathematics course designed at Level 0 may be every bit as pedagogically sophisticated as a graduate engineering course operating at Level 6. Their educational purposes are simply different. One protects the development of foundational reasoning. The other assumes that reasoning has already been established and therefore designs an environment in which increasingly sophisticated AI collaboration supports advanced professional learning.

Neither level is inherently superior. The measure of excellence is how well the instructional design aligns with the learner's developmental needs, not how much AI a course incorporates.

Level 0 succeeds not because artificial intelligence is absent. It succeeds because faculty have intentionally identified a moment within the curriculum when independent cognitive performance is educationally indispensable. Once that developmental purpose has been achieved, however, the instructional question necessarily changes.

Students no longer need the same level of technological support. Instead, they need guidance in learning how to incorporate artificial intelligence honestly and responsibly into their academic work. The curriculum, therefore, moves naturally from preserving independent cognition to cultivating intellectual accountability.

Developmental Transition: Independence Before Augmentation

Level 0 is often described as the most restrictive level within AI-CAM. That description is technically accurate, but educationally incomplete. Restriction is not the defining characteristic of this level. Developmental sequencing is.

Faculty choose Level 0 because they recognize that certain forms of learning require direct evidence of independent cognition before technological augmentation becomes educationally appropriate. Students first develop foundational reasoning, analytical habits, and disciplinary judgment through their own intellectual effort. Only then can artificial intelligence become an educational partner rather than a substitute for learning.

Seen in this way, Level 0 is neither an argument against AI nor a permanent instructional posture. It is one carefully designed stage within a larger developmental sequence. Once students have demonstrated foundational competence, the educational challenge changes. Faculty no longer need to protect independent cognition. They begin teaching students how to acknowledge technological assistance openly while preserving intellectual responsibility.

That developmental transition leads naturally to Level 1.

Chapter 6: Building a Culture of Transparency - Level 1 - AI Permitted with Citation

Developmental Principle: *Intellectual accountability precedes sophisticated collaboration.*

Why Choose This Level?

If Level 0 is concerned with protecting foundational cognition, Level 1 is concerned with making intellectual assistance visible.

That shift reflects an important developmental transition. Faculty are no longer asking whether students possess the foundational competencies that require independent demonstration. Those competencies have been established, at least for the learning tasks under consideration. The educational question now takes a different form: How should students begin integrating artificial intelligence into their academic work without obscuring authorship, responsibility, or intellectual accountability?

Across higher education, one of the earliest responses to generative AI was simply to require students to cite it. The reasoning was understandable. Citation had long served as the mechanism by which scholars acknowledged others' contributions, and AI appeared to present another source that required attribution. Yet many institutions quickly discovered that citation alone did not solve the educational problem. Students could accurately disclose their use of AI while still relying on it uncritically. Conversely, some students could use AI responsibly yet remain uncertain about when disclosure was actually required. The issue, therefore, was never merely one of citation format. It was one of intellectual transparency.

Level 1 addresses that problem.

Its purpose is not primarily to teach students how to use artificial intelligence. Neither is it intended to transform the curriculum. Instead, it establishes the ethical habits that enable later developmental stages. Before students can learn to evaluate AI critically, collaborate with it responsibly, or integrate it into professional practice, they must first become accustomed to acknowledging its presence honestly.

Transparency is therefore the first habit of responsible AI engagement. This represents a subtle shift in a course's educational culture.

At Level 1, AI is no longer absent, but neither is it invisible. Students are expected to disclose where and how it contributed to their work, not because disclosure is an end in itself, but because intellectual honesty depends upon making significant forms of assistance visible.

That expectation mirrors a much broader principle within academic life.

When students disclose their use of AI, they are not confessing to misconduct. They are documenting part of the intellectual process that produced the work. The disclosure itself communicates something important: this assignment emerged through a combination of human judgment and technological assistance, and the student is prepared to identify where those interactions occurred.

One unintended consequence of early institutional AI bans was that they often pushed AI use into a hidden curriculum. Students continued experimenting with emerging technologies because they recognized their potential value, but they did so quietly. Faculty, in turn, frequently suspected AI use without possessing sufficient evidence to distinguish appropriate assistance from inappropriate substitution. Both groups became participants in a system characterized more by mutual uncertainty than by educational clarity.

Rather than pretending AI is absent, a Level 1 course openly acknowledges its existence. More importantly, it invites conversation about it. Once AI use becomes visible, instructors gain opportunities that simply do not exist when students feel compelled to conceal their interactions with the technology. Faculty can ask why a student chose to use AI for one task rather than another. They can discuss whether the technology genuinely strengthened the students' thinking or merely accelerated routine work. They can explore the limitations of AI-generated responses without immediately placing students on the defensive.

At first glance, it appears modest. The curriculum changes very little. Assignments remain largely familiar. Learning outcomes continue emphasizing disciplinary knowledge rather than AI literacy. Compared with later levels, the instructional transformation seems minimal. Its significance, however, lies elsewhere.

Level 1 changes the culture of learning before it changes the curriculum.

Across institutions, faculty often discover that requiring disclosure alters student behavior in unexpected ways. Students who know they will describe how AI contributed to their work are often more selective about when to use it. They begin distinguishing between assistance that genuinely supports learning and assistance that merely bypasses intellectual effort. Questions that previously remained invisible become subjects of reflection.

- Did the AI simply organize my ideas, or did it shape the argument itself?
- Could I explain this concept without the AI's help?
- Did I verify the information it provided?
- At what point does assistance become substitution?

These are precisely the kinds of questions that responsible AI literacy requires. Yet they emerge naturally only after students begin viewing AI use as something worthy of reflection rather than concealment. This observation points toward an important curriculum principle.

Educational development often begins with awareness before it proceeds to mastery.

Students rarely become sophisticated writers simply by producing better essays. They become sophisticated writers by understanding how writing works. They learn to recognize their own habits, identify weaknesses, revise intentionally, and evaluate their decisions critically. Similar patterns appear in scientific reasoning, clinical judgment, artistic practice, and virtually every other domain of higher education.

Level 1 cultivates the same awareness regarding artificial intelligence. Students begin paying attention to their own interactions with technology. They notice when AI contributes meaningfully to learning and when it offers little more than superficial convenience. They begin to recognize that using AI involves a series of decisions requiring judgment rather than passive acceptance.

Those habits will matter more as professional environments move rapidly toward expectations of documented AI use rather than invisible AI use. Attorneys will increasingly disclose the use of AI-assisted legal drafting. Journalists already document AI participation in reporting. Healthcare professionals must identify decision-support systems that contributed to clinical recommendations. Business leaders are being asked to explain how AI influenced organizational decisions. Across professions, transparency is becoming an essential component of responsible technological practice.

Higher education should prepare students for that reality. The objective, however, is intellectual formation, not simply professional preparation.

Students who learn to acknowledge AI honestly are also learning something more fundamental: that authorship is defined less by producing words on a page than by assuming responsibility for the thinking those words represent. For that reason, faculty should not think of Level 1 primarily as a policy requiring citation. They should think of it as the point at which students begin developing a habit of intellectual accountability.

What Successful Implementation Looks Like

Successful Level 1 implementation is often less dramatic than faculty expect. Unlike the higher AI-CAM levels, it does not require major redesign of assignments, new learning outcomes, or extensive assessment revisions. In many respects, the course remains recognizably the same. What changes is the intellectual culture surrounding student work. Artificial intelligence is no longer treated as something that either exists outside the classroom or must remain hidden from it. Instead, it becomes an acknowledged element of the student's academic process.

Because Level 1 is developmental, its success should not be measured by how frequently students use AI. Nor should it be measured by how effectively they use it. At this stage, the educational objective is much more modest and, in many ways, more important. Students are learning that intellectual work includes the responsibility to disclose significant forms of assistance honestly and consistently. Transparency becomes part of scholarly practice rather than an exception to it.

The assignment remains fundamentally about the discipline. Artificial intelligence simply becomes one resource students may choose to incorporate into their work, provided they do so transparently. A student may use AI to organize preliminary ideas before drafting an essay, refine a paragraph's clarity, or generate questions to study difficult material. Another student may choose not to use AI at all. Either approach is entirely consistent with Level 1 because the educational objective is intellectual honesty, not technological proficiency.

Faculty should therefore communicate clearly where AI assistance is appropriate and where independent work remains essential. These expectations need not become exhaustive. In fact, one of the strengths of Level 1 is that it avoids attempting to regulate every conceivable interaction with AI. Instead, instructors identify broad principles that align with the course's learning objectives. Students understand that certain forms of assistance are acceptable, others are not, and that uncertainty should be resolved through conversation rather than assumption.

Assessment changes very little. This is intentional. What does change is that transparency becomes visible within the assessment process. This does not require a separate grading category devoted to AI use. In many cases, a brief disclosure accompanying the assignment provides all the information faculty need.

The central criteria continue to evaluate disciplinary competence. A history instructor assesses historical reasoning. A biology professor evaluates scientific understanding. A philosophy instructor grades the quality of argumentation. Artificial intelligence is not itself the object of evaluation.

More importantly, those disclosures create opportunities for meaningful instructional conversations. An instructor reading that a student used AI to improve organization may ask why organization proved difficult. Another student who reports using AI to summarize an assigned reading provides an opportunity to discuss the strengths and limitations of relying upon generated summaries rather than direct engagement with the text. The disclosure is valuable not because it documents technology but because it reveals aspects of the student's learning process that would otherwise remain invisible.

One of the early mistakes many institutions made was assuming that transparency required elaborate documentation systems. Some students were asked to submit every prompt they entered into an AI platform. Others were expected to identify every sentence influenced by AI or preserve complete transcripts of every interaction. Although well-intentioned, these approaches often produced more administrative work than educational value. Students became preoccupied with documenting AI rather than reflecting upon it.

Successful Level 1 implementation takes a different approach.

The disclosure should answer only those questions necessary to make AI participation visible.

A model of that minimal disclosure might read: "I used ChatGPT to help reorganize the second and third paragraphs of this essay and to check my citations for formatting accuracy. I reviewed and revised every suggested change before submitting." Nothing about that statement requires an elaborate log or a separate template. It names the tool, identifies the general task, and confirms that the student remained the evaluating authority over what the tool produced, which is the complete range of information Level 1 disclosure exists to capture.

- Which system, if any, was used?
- For what purpose?
- To what extent did its contributions remain in the final submission?

Those few pieces of information are usually sufficient. They provide instructors with meaningful context while preserving the emphasis on disciplinary learning rather than bureaucratic compliance.

Equally important is how faculty respond to those disclosures.

If students come to believe that every acknowledgment of AI use invites suspicion or penalty, transparency quickly becomes performative rather than genuine. Faculty should instead treat disclosure as an expected component of scholarly communication. Students who honestly report AI use should find that disclosure itself is entirely unremarkable. The conversation naturally shifts to whether the technology supported learning appropriately rather than whether it was used at all.

At Level 1, that judgment remains relatively simple. Students are learning to think consciously about when AI enters their academic work and how they should acknowledge its presence. Yet even this modest habit represents meaningful intellectual growth because it moves students beyond unreflective use of technology toward intentional decision-making.

Where This Level Fails

Like every level within the AI-CAM framework, Level 1 succeeds only when its developmental purpose remains clear. The educational objective is the cultivation of intellectual accountability - citation is merely its outward form. When that distinction is forgotten, the level begins to drift away from the role it was designed to serve.

The most common failure is surprisingly simple. Transparency becomes compliance.

Across institutions, I have seen faculty devote considerable attention to developing AI citation requirements while investing very little attention in what those disclosures actually reveal about student learning. Students dutifully complete disclosure statements because they are required to. Faculty glance at them briefly—or not at all—and then proceed directly to grading the assignment. Over time, disclosure becomes another administrative form attached to student work rather than an opportunity for educational reflection.

Students cite sources because scholarly conventions require it. AI disclosure can easily become absorbed into that same mindset. Yet the analogy is incomplete. Traditional citations primarily acknowledge intellectual debts. AI disclosures reveal something different. They make visible aspects of the student's decision-making process that would otherwise remain hidden. If faculty never engage those disclosures as part of the learning conversation, one of the principal educational benefits of Level 1 has been lost.

Transparency should generate discussion.

It should prompt questions about why students chose to use AI in particular ways, what they found helpful, where the technology proved inadequate, and how their own thinking developed through the process. Those conversations gradually cultivate the reflective habits that later levels of AI-CAM depend upon.

A second failure occurs when institutions mistake transparency for AI literacy.

This misunderstanding has become increasingly common as colleges and universities rush to establish AI policies. Requiring students to disclose their use of AI certainly promotes honesty. It does not necessarily promote discernment.

Students may become highly skilled at documenting AI participation while remaining remarkably poor at evaluating the quality of AI-generated work. They may accurately identify every interaction with the technology yet possess little understanding of when those interactions strengthen learning and when they undermine it.

Transparency creates the conditions for responsible AI use. It does not, by itself, produce responsible AI use.

Another institutional failure emerges when disclosure requirements become unnecessarily complicated.

During the earliest institutional responses to generative AI, some policies required students to preserve every prompt, document every interaction, identify every AI-generated sentence, or produce lengthy appendices detailing the complete history of their work. Although such requirements were generally motivated by legitimate concerns about academic integrity, they often produced unintended educational consequences.

Students became preoccupied with documenting technology rather than reflecting upon learning.

Faculty spent an increasing amount of time reviewing procedural records that contributed relatively little to the understanding of student thinking. The administrative burden grew while the educational value remained limited.

The disclosure should be sufficient to make AI participation visible without becoming the assignment itself. Transparency is valuable because it supports learning, not because it generates additional paperwork.

There is also a subtler failure that emerges in some institutional cultures. Faculty unintentionally communicate that disclosure is equivalent to suspicion.

Students quickly learn to interpret AI acknowledgments as confessions rather than ordinary components of scholarly communication. Every disclosure appears to invite additional scrutiny. Every mention of AI becomes something to justify or defend. Under these conditions, transparency no longer strengthens trust. It simply replaces hidden AI use with reluctant disclosure.

That is precisely the opposite of what Level 1 intends to accomplish.

The educational culture should communicate that responsible disclosure is entirely normal. Faculty are interested in understanding the student's learning process, not in searching for evidence of misconduct. When transparency becomes routine rather than exceptional, students begin to view AI use as another instructional decision that requires thoughtful judgment, rather than as something best concealed whenever possible.

Perhaps the most noticeable failure, however, occurs when institutions remain permanently at Level 1.

This often happens because transparency feels like a complete solution. Faculty develop citation policies, revise syllabi, establish disclosure statements, and understandably conclude that the educational challenge has largely been addressed.

In reality, the developmental work has only begun. Students who honestly disclose AI use still need guidance on where AI belongs in the learning process. They need opportunities to distinguish between appropriate support and inappropriate substitution. They need structured experiences that explain why some forms of AI assistance strengthen learning while others do not.

Transparency alone cannot answer those questions.

Eventually, the curriculum must move beyond asking students to acknowledge AI toward helping them understand how AI should participate in their own intellectual development. That transition requires faculty to think differently about instructional design.

That distinction becomes the defining educational question of Level 2.

Developmental Transition: Transparency Before Judgment

Level 1 establishes one of the most important habits students can develop in an AI-mediated learning environment: intellectual transparency. Before students can evaluate artificial intelligence wisely, they must first become accustomed to acknowledging its presence honestly.

Disclosure, however, is only the beginning of AI literacy. Transparency creates visibility, but visibility alone does not produce discernment. Students still need to learn where AI appropriately contributes to learning and where its participation begins to replace the intellectual work that education exists to cultivate.

The next developmental task, therefore, moves beyond acknowledgment toward instructional judgment. Students begin learning not simply to disclose AI use but to determine when it genuinely strengthens learning.

Chapter 7: AI as Learning Support - Level 2 - AI Encouraged for Support Tasks

Developmental Principle: *Not every cognitive task contributes equally to learning.*

Why Choose This Level?

By the time students reach Level 2, the educational conversation shifts significantly. The central concern is no longer whether artificial intelligence should remain hidden, nor whether students should disclose its use. Those habits have already begun to develop. Instead, faculty confront a more nuanced instructional question: Which aspects of learning should students continue to perform independently, and which aspects can appropriately be supported by artificial intelligence without compromising intellectual development?

Every course requires students to perform a wide variety of cognitive tasks, yet not all of those tasks serve the same educational purpose. Some activities prepare students for learning. Others constitute the learning itself. Effective teaching has always distinguished between the two, even if faculty have not always described the distinction explicitly.

Consider a typical writing assignment. Before students construct an argument, they may spend considerable time organizing notes, generating possible thesis statements, identifying recurring themes within their sources, or outlining a logical sequence for their paper. These preparatory activities are certainly valuable. They help students approach the larger intellectual task with greater clarity. Yet the assignment's educational objective is rarely the production of an outline. It is the construction of a coherent argument supported by evidence and disciplined reasoning.

The same distinction appears across the curriculum.

Biology students organize terminology before learning physiological relationships. Students in history assemble timelines before interpreting historical causation. Business students summarize financial reports before evaluating strategic alternatives. Nursing students review disease processes before making clinical judgments. In each case, preparatory work supports learning, but it is not identical to the higher-order reasoning that faculty ultimately hope to cultivate.

Level 2 emerges from this observation.

Its pedagogical logic rests on the recognition that artificial intelligence can sometimes reduce the cognitive effort of preparatory activities while leaving the essential disciplinary work firmly in the learner's hands.

This is important because discussions of AI often assume that all forms of cognitive effort possess equal educational value. They do not.

The question is not whether AI saves time. Saving time has no inherent educational value. The more important question is what students do with the intellectual time and energy that AI makes available. If the technology simply allows students to finish assignments more quickly, little has been gained. If, however, it enables them to devote greater attention to analysis, synthesis, evaluation, and reflection, then AI has begun serving a genuinely pedagogical purpose.

Seen from this perspective, Level 2 is fundamentally about allocating cognitive effort.

Faculty intentionally identify aspects of learning that can be supported without diminishing the developmental work the course is designed to accomplish. Artificial intelligence becomes one instructional scaffold among many. Like every scaffold, it exists not to replace the structure being built but to support its construction until greater competence develops.

The concept of scaffolding has long occupied an important place within educational theory. Effective instruction provides temporary support while students acquire increasingly sophisticated capabilities. As competence grows, those supports gradually recede as the learner internalizes the underlying knowledge and skills. The value of Artificial Intelligence depends not on how much work it performs, but on whether it strengthens the learner's capacity for independent disciplinary thinking.

That is particularly important because AI possesses a quality unlike most previous educational technologies. It can appear to perform intellectual work rather than merely support it.

An outline generated by AI may look remarkably similar to one developed independently by a student. A study guide may appear comprehensive and accurate. A summary may read fluently enough that students mistake familiarity with the summary for understanding of the underlying material. This apparent competence creates a unique instructional challenge. Faculty must continually distinguish between activities that prepare students to think and activities that require students to do the thinking themselves.

In an introductory history course, asking AI to interpret primary sources would likely undermine the assignment's central purpose. In an advanced historiography seminar, however, comparing AI-generated interpretations with established historical scholarship might become a valuable preparatory exercise before students formulate their own analysis. Similarly, an AI-generated study guide may appropriately support preparation for a biology examination, while an AI-generated laboratory interpretation would substitute for precisely the reasoning students are expected to develop.

This variability explains why Level 2 cannot be reduced to a list of permitted and prohibited tasks. The appropriate use of AI depends upon what the instructor is trying to teach.

Across institutions, I have found that faculty often reach Level 2 after recognizing that not every assignment warrants the same AI policy. Earlier conversations frequently revolved around broad institutional questions: Should students be allowed to use AI? Should it be prohibited? Over time, those questions gradually became more specific. Faculty began asking whether AI should assist with brainstorming but not analysis, organization but not interpretation, review but not evaluation. The discussion shifted away from technology and toward pedagogy.

One of the challenges many learners face when first encountering AI is that the technology appears capable of assisting with almost everything. Without guidance, they naturally assume that more assistance must be better. Level 2 introduces a more disciplined understanding. Students discover that declining AI assistance can sometimes be just as intellectually important as accepting it.

This is the beginning of discernment. Students are no longer making decisions solely about whether to use AI. They are making decisions about *why* they are using it and whether that use strengthens or weakens the learning process. Such discernment marks an important stage in intellectual development because it recognizes that technology is not educationally neutral. Every instructional choice—including the choice to use artificial intelligence—shapes where attention is directed, which habits of mind are reinforced, and how disciplinary competence develops over time.

Level 2 represents the first stage at which artificial intelligence begins to function intentionally in the instructional design of a course. The technology is no longer simply acknowledged through disclosure. It is deliberately positioned to support learning in ways that remain subordinate to the curriculum's larger developmental goals.

As students become increasingly intentional about where AI belongs within their own learning process, a new educational possibility emerges. Faculty are no longer limited to permitting or encouraging AI support. They can begin asking students to examine AI itself—to evaluate its strengths, identify its limitations, and compare its reasoning with disciplinary standards.

What Successful Implementation Looks Like

Successful Level 2 implementation is characterized by intentionality. Faculty are no longer making a binary decision about whether AI is permitted. They are making instructional decisions about where AI contributes to learning and where it does not. That distinction should be evident throughout the course's design. Students should be able to understand not only *what* they are permitted to do with AI but also *why* those uses are educationally appropriate.

This represents an important shift in the relationship between technology and pedagogy. In Level 1, transparency was the primary instructional objective. AI was acknowledged, but it remained largely peripheral to the learning process. At Level 2, AI begins serving the curriculum directly. It supports learning activities that prepare students for deeper disciplinary work while leaving the course's central intellectual responsibilities unchanged.

Faculty, therefore, begin designing assignments with two distinct questions in mind. First, where are students investing substantial effort in tasks that prepare them for learning but are not themselves the primary learning objective? Second, would carefully structured AI support allow students to devote more time to the kinds of thinking the discipline actually values?

Those questions often lead to surprisingly different assignment designs.

Consider a research paper in an introductory political science course. Traditionally, students may spend several hours organizing notes from articles, identifying recurring themes, and constructing a preliminary outline before beginning to write. None of those activities is unimportant. Yet neither is the principal objective of the assignment. The educational goal is to analyze political arguments, evaluate evidence, and construct a persuasive interpretation. An instructor operating at Level 2 might therefore encourage students to use AI to organize research notes or suggest possible organizational frameworks while making it clear that the analytical argument itself must emerge from the student's own disciplinary reasoning.

The technology has not replaced learning. It has simply reduced the time devoted to preparatory work, allowing more attention to be directed toward interpretation, synthesis, and analysis. The same principle applies across disciplines.

Students should never be left wondering why AI is encouraged for one activity but discouraged for another. Faculty should explain the developmental reasoning behind those decisions.

Assessment practices likewise reflect the developmental purpose of Level 2.

The primary object of evaluation remains the student's disciplinary understanding. This means assessment increasingly focuses on evidence that students engaged thoughtfully with AI-generated support rather than simply accepting it.

A study guide generated by artificial intelligence, for example, becomes educationally meaningful when students correct inaccuracies, expand incomplete explanations, identify concepts requiring additional study, or annotate connections that the AI failed to recognize. Likewise, an AI-generated outline acquires instructional value only when students reorganize it, reject portions that do not fit their argument, or strengthen its structure through independent disciplinary judgment.

In each case, faculty are assessing not the quality of the AI's work but the quality of the student's interaction with it.

That distinction becomes correspondingly important as AI systems continue to improve. Eventually, the technology may produce organizational materials that are indistinguishable from those created by experienced students. Yet educationally, the question remains unchanged. Did the student think critically about the support provided, or did they accept it without reflection?

Because AI now plays an intentional role within aspects of the learning process, students should identify how it contributed to their preparation. These disclosures need not become elaborate. A brief statement indicating that AI assisted with brainstorming, organization, vocabulary review, or study guide development is generally sufficient. The purpose remains transparency rather than documentation for its own sake.

At this level, a disclosure might read: "I used an AI tool to brainstorm three possible thesis directions and to generate a first-pass outline for this paper. I selected one direction, set aside the outline's proposed evidence in favor of my own research, and restructured the argument around a claim the AI had not suggested." The added detail here, compared to a Level 1 disclosure, reflects the wider range of tasks AI is now permitted to support, but the statement is still short enough to write in a few sentences and does not require a separate log.

Students become increasingly aware of where AI genuinely helped them and where it merely appeared productive. Those insights often become valuable teaching moments. A student who relied heavily on AI-generated summaries but struggled to analyze primary texts may discover that preparation cannot substitute for direct engagement with disciplinary material. Another who used AI to organize complex notes may recognize that the additional time available allowed for much deeper analysis than previous assignments had permitted.

These observations help students develop an increasingly sophisticated understanding of their own learning processes.

Perhaps the most remarkable characteristic of successful Level 2 implementation is that students begin exercising instructional judgment themselves.

Initially, faculty establish the boundaries. They explain where AI belongs and where it does not. Over time, however, students begin asking the same questions independently. Is this a task where AI will genuinely strengthen my learning? Am I asking the technology to prepare me for thinking or to do the thinking on my behalf? Will using AI here improve my understanding, or will it merely improve the appearance of my work?

That habit of self-regulation is one of the most important outcomes of Level 2 because it prepares students for a more demanding stage of learning. Once they understand where AI appropriately supports learning, they are ready to begin investigating AI itself—its strengths, weaknesses, assumptions, and limitations.

Where This Level Fails

The effectiveness of Level 2 depends upon maintaining a clear distinction between instructional support and intellectual substitution. Faculty choose this level because they have concluded that certain aspects of learning can be assisted by artificial intelligence without compromising the developmental work the course is intended to accomplish. When that distinction begins to erode, the educational logic of the level erodes with it.

The most common failure is that support gradually becomes substitution. This rarely happens through a deliberate curricular decision. More often, it occurs incrementally.

Faculty initially encourage AI for brainstorming. Students soon begin to ask whether it can also generate preliminary outlines. Before long, those outlines become partial drafts, and partial drafts quietly become complete first drafts requiring only minor revision. Each step appears reasonable in isolation. Collectively, however, they shift AI from supporting the learning process to performing the very intellectual work students were expected to do themselves.

What makes this progression particularly difficult to recognize is that the quality of student work often appears to improve. Yet beneath that improvement may lie an important developmental question: Has the student's thinking become stronger, or has the technology simply become more involved? Surface performance is no longer a reliable indicator of intellectual growth.

A second failure occurs when efficiency becomes confused with learning.

One of the genuine advantages of artificial intelligence is its ability to reduce time spent on repetitive or organizational tasks. Faculty frequently observe that students can prepare study materials, organize research notes, or review foundational concepts much more efficiently than before. Those efficiencies are real. They are not, however, educational outcomes in themselves.

The educational value lies in what students do with the time and cognitive energy that have been freed. Across institutions, I have seen two very different patterns emerge.

In one, students use AI-supported preparation to devote substantially more attention to analysis, interpretation, problem solving, and discussion. The technology creates space for deeper engagement with disciplinary ideas.

In the other, and more frequent, students simply complete the assignment more quickly. The course becomes more efficient. Learning does not necessarily become deeper.

Efficiency is valuable only when it serves intellectual formation.

Another recurring failure emerges when faculty assume that students already know how to use AI appropriately for learning. This assumption has become increasingly common because today's students appear comfortable with digital technologies. Familiarity, however, should not be confused with educational judgment.

Students often arrive possessing highly uneven experiences with artificial intelligence. If faculty simply encourage AI-supported preparation without explaining why certain uses are educationally appropriate, the strongest students often become even stronger, while less experienced students continue using AI in ways that contribute relatively little to their intellectual development. Level 2, therefore, requires instruction as well as permission.

There is also another institutional failure that deserves attention. Faculty sometimes begin organizing assignments around what AI does well rather than around what students most need to learn.

At first glance, this may appear sensible. If AI summarizes information efficiently, why not redesign courses to take advantage of that capability? Yet curriculum has never been organized around the strengths of instructional technologies. It has always been organized around learners' developmental needs.

When technology begins determining instructional priorities, curriculum gradually becomes reactive rather than intentional. Faculty start asking, "What can AI do?" instead of the more important question, "What kind of thinking are we trying to cultivate?"

Finally, a failure point occurs when institutions remain satisfied with Level 2.

Because AI is now being used productively within learning activities, it is tempting to conclude that meaningful integration has been achieved. Students appear comfortable with the technology. Faculty observe improvements in preparation and organization. The course functions well.

Yet an important educational opportunity remains unrealized. Students have learned where AI can support learning. They have not yet learned to evaluate AI critically. They know how to use it. They do not yet know how to supervise it.

That distinction becomes increasingly important as artificial intelligence grows more capable. The more fluent these technologies become, the more sophisticated the judgment required to use them well. Students who understand where AI is useful but lack the ability to recognize its limitations remain vulnerable to precisely the kinds of overconfidence that professional practice cannot afford.

Eventually, therefore, the curriculum must ask students to do something more demanding than use AI appropriately. It must ask them to evaluate AI itself.

That shift marks one of the most important transitions within the AI-CAM framework. The student moves from being an informed user of artificial intelligence to a thoughtful evaluator.

That is the developmental purpose of Level 3.

Developmental Transition: Support Before Evaluation

Level 2 reminds us that not every cognitive task contributes equally to learning. Artificial intelligence can often support preparation without replacing the disciplinary reasoning that remains central to intellectual development.

Yet appropriate use is only one stage of educational maturity. Students who understand where AI belongs within their learning still need to determine whether its contributions deserve their confidence. Responsible use eventually gives way to critical evaluation.

The curriculum, therefore, progresses from using AI thoughtfully to examining AI critically. Students begin exercising the habits of disciplinary judgment that distinguish informed users from thoughtful evaluators.

That developmental progression defines Level 3.

Readers interested in seeing this level implemented in an authentic institutional setting may wish to consult **Appendix A**, which presents a detailed case study illustrating how one faculty member redesigned a course using the developmental principles described in this chapter. Rather than serving as a model to be copied directly, the case is intended to demonstrate the reasoning that connects developmental purpose, course design, assessment, and AI integration within a specific educational context.

Chapter 8: Learning to Critique AI - Level 3 - AI-Required Assignment(s)

Developmental Principle: *Students learn to evaluate artificial intelligence only after they have learned to use it responsibly.*

Why Choose This Level?

The transition from Level 2 to Level 3 represents one of the most significant shifts within the AI-Course Application Matrix. Up to this point, artificial intelligence has occupied a supporting role within the learning environment. Students have learned to acknowledge its use transparently and to employ it selectively for activities that prepare them for deeper disciplinary work. AI has served the learning process, but it has not yet become part of what students are expected to learn.

Level 3 changes that relationship. Artificial intelligence becomes an intentional object of instruction.

This shift reflects an important principle of educational development. Students should not be asked to critique a technology before they have developed sufficient familiarity with it to understand how it works in their own learning. Critical evaluation presupposes experience. Before students can recognize the strengths and weaknesses of AI-generated responses, they must encounter them in authentic academic work. Before they can identify bias, hallucination, overconfidence, or shallow reasoning, they must first understand what competent disciplinary reasoning actually looks like. That sequence matters.

Across higher education, there has been considerable enthusiasm for teaching students to "critically evaluate AI." While the objective is entirely appropriate, the timing is often overlooked. Critical evaluation is an intermediate competency, not a beginning one. Students who have never worked thoughtfully with AI possess little basis for judging when its reasoning succeeds or fails. They frequently oscillate between two equally unproductive positions. Some assume AI is inherently trustworthy because its responses appear confident and articulate. Others dismiss it entirely because they have encountered obvious errors. Neither response reflects disciplined judgment.

This is the point in the developmental sequence where AI itself enters the curriculum—not as a technological novelty, but as a legitimate object of disciplinary analysis.

The purpose of a Level 3 assignment is not to teach students more about artificial intelligence than about their discipline. Quite the opposite. AI becomes valuable precisely because it provides a new context for disciplinary thinking. Students evaluate AI-generated arguments by applying critical reasoning from their academic context. The technology becomes a mirror against which disciplinary competence is demonstrated.

Artificial intelligence becomes valuable because it creates opportunities for students to exercise disciplinary judgment under conditions that increasingly resemble the professional environments they will eventually enter. Rather than replacing disciplinary rigor, AI raises new questions that require even greater disciplinary sophistication to answer well.

Graduates entering professional practice are unlikely to encounter workplaces without AI. They are far more likely to encounter environments in which AI routinely generates reports, summarizes research, recommends diagnoses, drafts legal language, analyzes financial data, or produces preliminary designs. Their professional value will therefore depend less on generating information than on evaluating it.

Higher education has traditionally emphasized the production of knowledge. Students write papers, solve problems, construct models, and formulate arguments because those activities cultivate disciplinary understanding. Artificial intelligence does not eliminate those educational purposes, but it does expand them. Students must now learn to evaluate knowledge that they did not produce themselves. They must distinguish between accurate reasoning and plausible reasoning, evidence-based conclusions and confident speculation, and disciplinary rigor and algorithmic fluency.

In many ways, the task resembles evaluating scholarly literature. Students must distinguish strong arguments from weak ones, well-supported conclusions from confident assertions, and genuine insight from plausible but incomplete analysis.

It requires habits of skepticism, verification, comparison, and reflective judgment that extend well beyond technological proficiency. Indeed, one recurring pattern I have observed in faculty development is that students who initially appear highly skilled with AI often struggle when asked to critically evaluate its outputs. They know how to obtain information quickly. They are much less certain how to determine whether that information deserves their confidence.

At Level 3, students begin asking different questions.

- Why did the AI reach this conclusion? And, is it valid?
- What assumptions shaped its response?
- Where does its reasoning depart from accepted disciplinary standards?
- How would an expert recognize the weaknesses in this analysis?

Notice that these are not questions about technology. They are questions about judgment.

The educational objective is, therefore, disciplinary literacy exercised within an AI-mediated environment, rather than technological literacy in the narrow sense of understanding AI systems. Students learn to think *through* their discipline about artificial intelligence rather than merely learning *about* it.

Faculty choose this level because certain learning outcomes cannot be achieved simply by permitting or encouraging AI use. If students are expected to become thoughtful supervisors of increasingly capable technologies, they must practice supervising them while the consequences of errors remain educational rather than professional. The classroom provides precisely that environment. AI-generated mistakes become opportunities for learning rather than sources of organizational or professional failure.

Across disciplines, this is often one of the most intellectually engaging stages of AI integration. Students are frequently surprised by the limitations of systems they previously regarded as highly authoritative. They discover that AI can generate persuasive yet historically inaccurate narratives, statistically sophisticated yet methodologically flawed analyses, legally coherent yet procedurally incomplete arguments, or clinically plausible recommendations that overlook essential patient information. These discoveries do more than reveal AI's weaknesses. They deepen students' understanding of the discipline itself because identifying those weaknesses requires increasingly sophisticated disciplinary reasoning.

In many respects, Level 3 transforms AI into an educational case study. The technology provides authentic material for students to exercise the habits of mind their discipline values most. AI creates new opportunities to demonstrate disciplinary competence in contemporary conditions.

This is why Level 3 occupies such an important position within the developmental sequence. Students are no longer merely integrating AI into their learning. They are learning to evaluate AI with the intellectual standards of their discipline.

Once that capacity begins to develop, another possibility emerges. Artificial intelligence is no longer simply something students can critique effectively. It becomes a competency that can itself be embedded within the learning outcomes of a course or program. Institutions can then move beyond isolated AI assignments toward curricula in which AI literacy is intentionally assessed as part of disciplinary education.

What Successful Implementation Looks Like

Successful Level 3 implementation is defined by a single central characteristic: the assignment requires students to exercise disciplinary judgment when evaluating artificial intelligence. AI is no longer optional, but it is not the primary subject of the course either. Instead, it serves as an instructional catalyst, making disciplinary thinking more visible.

The most successful Level 3 designs, therefore, begin with disciplinary learning outcomes rather than technological capabilities. Faculty first identify a concept, method, or form of reasoning that students have already begun to master. They then create an assignment in which AI produces work that students must evaluate using those disciplinary standards.

A history instructor might ask students to compare an AI-generated interpretation of a historical event with primary source evidence and established historical scholarship. A business professor may require students to critique an AI-produced strategic analysis by identifying unsupported assumptions or missing market variables. Students in a nursing program may review AI-generated clinical recommendations and identify where patient-specific information warrants a different course of action. Engineering students may analyze AI-generated design proposals, identifying technical limitations that the system failed to recognize.

Although these assignments differ considerably, they share the same instructional structure. The student's learning is demonstrated through evaluation rather than acceptance. Artificial intelligence provides the material for analysis, but disciplinary reasoning remains the mechanism through which learning is assessed.

Students quickly discover that AI can produce work that is both impressive and incomplete. A response may be fluent but historically inaccurate. A recommendation may appear logical while overlooking essential contextual information. A legal summary may accurately describe precedent while misapplying procedural requirements. These inconsistencies become educationally valuable because students are expected to recognize them.

Faculty frequently report that assignments of this kind produce unusually rich classroom discussions.

Students who had previously regarded AI as either unquestionably reliable or fundamentally unreliable begin developing more nuanced judgments. They recognize that the technology performs remarkably well within certain boundaries, but struggles when contextual interpretation, disciplinary expertise, or professional judgment is required. Those observations emerge not because the instructor lectures on AI's limitations, but because students discover them through disciplined analysis.

Assessment at Level 3, therefore, expands in an important way.

Faculty continue to evaluate disciplinary competence, but now assess students' ability to apply it to the evaluation of AI-generated work. The assignment is successful not because students identify every error the AI produces, but because they demonstrate thoughtful, evidence-based reasoning in explaining why particular responses are convincing, incomplete, misleading, or inconsistent with accepted disciplinary standards. The educational objective, then, is not simply "finding mistakes."

Students sometimes approach early AI evaluation assignments as though the instructor expects them to prove the technology wrong. That quickly becomes an exercise in error hunting rather than critical thinking. A successful Level 3 assessment rewards careful reasoning, regardless of the conclusion students reach. There will be occasions when AI produces analyses that are entirely appropriate. There will be others that require major revision. In both cases, the quality of the student's judgment—not the number of errors identified—becomes the object of evaluation.

Faculty, therefore, consider questions such as:

- Can the student explain *why* an AI-generated conclusion is persuasive or problematic?
- Can they distinguish factual accuracy from disciplinary adequacy?
- Can they support their evaluation using accepted evidence and methods within the field?
- Can they recognize the difference between superficial fluency and genuine expertise?

Disclosure practices also evolve at this level.

Earlier levels asked students primarily to acknowledge whether AI had contributed to their work. At Level 3, disclosure becomes part of the assignment itself because AI interaction is intentionally structured. Students should identify the prompts they used, summarize the responses they received, and explain how those responses informed their subsequent evaluation. The objective is not exhaustive documentation but intellectual transparency. Faculty should be able to understand the sequence of interactions that led to the student's analysis.

A student meeting that expectation might document something like this: "Prompt 1 asked the AI to summarize the causes of the 2008 financial crisis; it identified subprime lending, securitization, and regulatory gaps. Prompt 2 asked which of these three causes economists most often treat as primary; the AI cited securitization practices, without naming specific sources. I cross-checked this claim against two assigned readings and found only partial support; one author treated regulatory failure as the more fundamental cause. My final analysis reflects that disagreement rather than the AI's original framing." This is what intellectual transparency looks like in practice at Level 3: not a transcript of everything the AI produced, but a record of the reasoning that carried the student from the AI's output to their own conclusion. Readers looking for a longer illustration of this same disclosure practice applied at book length rather than assignment length will find one in this book's own Preface, in the note on the manuscript's preparation.

Just as importantly, students should be encouraged to reflect briefly on the evaluation process itself.

- What surprised them?
- Where did AI perform better than expected?
- Where did it fail?
- How did the exercise change their understanding of the discipline?

These reflections need not be lengthy, nor should they overshadow the disciplinary work. Their value lies in helping students recognize that evaluating AI requires many of the same habits of mind that characterize expert practice within their field. Verification, skepticism, comparison, contextual reasoning, and careful interpretation are not new competencies introduced by artificial intelligence. They are longstanding disciplinary virtues now being exercised in a contemporary context.

Perhaps the most important indicator of successful Level 3 implementation is a subtle change in how students approach AI beyond the assignment itself.

Faculty often observe that students begin questioning AI outputs much more naturally in subsequent coursework. They verify sources more consistently. They compare generated explanations against textbooks or primary literature. They become less impressed by confident language and more attentive to underlying evidence. Students begin interacting with AI more like experts than novices.

That change represents genuine educational development. Students are no longer learning merely to use artificial intelligence. They are learning to supervise it.

Where This Level Fails

Level 3 succeeds only when faculty remember why AI has been included in the assignment. The purpose is not technological exposure; it is a disciplinary judgment. Artificial intelligence enhances the learning experience by creating authentic opportunities for students to evaluate ideas, methods, and conclusions using the discipline's intellectual standards. When that purpose becomes obscured, the level's educational value diminishes rapidly.

The most common failure occurs when the assignment gradually shifts from the discipline to AI.

This is an understandable temptation. Artificial intelligence is novel, rapidly evolving, and intellectually fascinating. Faculty naturally become interested in comparing different platforms, experimenting with prompting strategies, or exploring the surprising capabilities of emerging models. Students often find these activities engaging as well. Yet enthusiasm for the technology can quietly displace the educational purpose that originally justified its introduction.

When the discipline slowly moves to the margins. Artificial intelligence becomes the curriculum rather than the context in which disciplinary thinking is exercised.

A second failure emerges when faculty unintentionally reward technological sophistication rather than intellectual judgment.

Students quickly recognize what instructors value.

If assignments consistently praise elaborate prompting strategies while paying comparatively little attention to the quality of disciplinary analysis, students naturally conclude that success depends upon becoming more technically proficient with AI. The technology gradually becomes the focus of their effort.

This outcome reflects an important shift in assessment.

The strongest Level 3 assignments reward students for explaining *why* an AI-generated response succeeds or fails in accordance with disciplinary standards. The weakest reward students simply for obtaining interesting AI outputs. In the former, AI creates opportunities for deeper thinking. In the latter, AI becomes little more than an entertaining instructional device.

Another failure occurs when evaluation becomes error hunting.

Students sometimes assume that the purpose of a Level 3 assignment is to prove AI wrong. Faculty may unintentionally reinforce this impression by selecting examples that contain obvious factual mistakes or exaggerated hallucinations. While such examples can be useful for introducing critical evaluation, they rarely represent the kinds of AI interactions graduates will encounter professionally.

Increasingly capable AI systems produce work that is often plausible, internally coherent, and substantially correct. Their limitations are frequently subtle rather than obvious. They omit important contextual information, overgeneralize from incomplete evidence, flatten disciplinary nuance, or present contested interpretations with unwarranted confidence. Recognizing these limitations requires considerably more disciplinary sophistication than identifying simple factual errors.

Students, therefore, need assignments that cultivate discernment rather than suspicion. The objective is not to teach that AI is unreliable. The objective is to teach that reliable professional judgment always requires evaluation, regardless of how convincing technological outputs may appear.

Institutional failure occurs when Level 3 remains confined to isolated assignments.

Faculty successfully design one thoughtful AI evaluation activity during the semester. Students perform well. The assignment is remembered positively. Yet nothing within the broader curriculum changes. AI evaluation remains an interesting exercise rather than becoming part of the program's educational commitments.

If faculty have concluded that graduates need the ability to evaluate artificial intelligence in their discipline, then that competency should eventually extend beyond isolated assignments. It should become part of what the curriculum intentionally promises to develop.

Developmental Transition: Evaluation Before Competency

Level 3 marks the point at which artificial intelligence becomes an object of disciplined inquiry. Students no longer interact with AI simply because it is available. They evaluate its reasoning, test its conclusions, and measure its performance against the intellectual standards of their discipline.

Eventually, however, isolated evaluation becomes insufficient. If graduates are expected to exercise these forms of judgment consistently in professional practice, AI literacy cannot remain confined to individual assignments. It must become part of the curriculum's explicit educational commitments.

The question, therefore, changes from whether students can evaluate AI to whether responsible AI judgment has become an essential component of disciplinary competence.

Readers interested in seeing this level implemented in an authentic institutional setting may wish to consult **Appendix A**, which presents a detailed case study illustrating how one faculty member redesigned a course using the developmental principles described in this chapter.

Chapter 9: AI Literacy as a Learning Outcome - Level 4 - AI Literacy Embedded in Learning Outcomes

Developmental Principle: *Professional competence requires measurable AI literacy.*

Why Choose This Level?

The movement from Level 3 to Level 4 marks an important transition in the educational purpose of AI integration. Up to this point, artificial intelligence has been introduced through individual assignments. Students have learned to disclose its use, employ it appropriately as a learning support, and evaluate its outputs critically within their discipline. AI has become part of selected learning activities, but it has not yet become part of what the curriculum explicitly promises students they will learn.

Level 4 changes that relationship. Artificial intelligence is no longer simply part of the instructional strategy. It becomes part of the intended educational outcome.

Every learning outcome conveys what an institution considers essential. Faculty include outcomes because they believe students should leave the course with specific forms of knowledge, habits of mind, or professional competencies. Learning outcomes, therefore, do more than organize assessment. They articulate the educational commitments of a curriculum. When AI literacy appears among those outcomes, the institution is making a public statement that responsible engagement with artificial intelligence has become part of disciplinary competence rather than an optional enrichment activity.

Across professions, artificial intelligence is becoming integrated into the ordinary work of analysis, communication, planning, diagnosis, design, and decision-making. Physicians encounter AI-assisted clinical recommendations. Attorneys review AI-supported legal research. Engineers employ increasingly sophisticated design systems. Business leaders interpret AI-generated market analyses. Journalists verify AI-assisted reporting. Educators themselves are learning to navigate classrooms in which students routinely interact with generative technologies.

Empirical evidence supports treating AI literacy as a multidimensional competency. Medina-Gual et al. (2025) distinguish among functional, technical, and socio-critical dimensions of AI literacy and find that these dimensions are related but distinct. In their study of 353 undergraduates at a private university in Mexico, only 2.6 percent demonstrated outstanding performance in the socio-critical dimension. Although the study's institutional context limits broad generalization, this finding underscores the need for explicit instruction in the ethical, social, and critical dimensions of AI use. Students may demonstrate functional competence with AI tools without possessing corresponding technical understanding or the ability to evaluate their ethical and social implications.

The growing presence of AI means that graduates will be expected not merely to operate technological systems but to supervise them responsibly. Their professional value will increasingly depend upon the ability to recognize where AI contributes productively, where it introduces risk, and where human judgment must ultimately prevail.

Level 4 expands the conversation from instructional design to curriculum design. Faculty are beginning to ask whether AI literacy should itself become part of what students are expected to know and demonstrate by the conclusion of the course.

Historically, professional education has evolved whenever new forms of knowledge became indispensable to competent practice. Information literacy gradually became embedded within general education because graduates needed to evaluate digital information critically. Statistical reasoning became increasingly common across disciplines because data-informed decision-making expanded beyond the sciences. Ethical reasoning moved from isolated philosophy courses into professional curricula because every discipline confronted more complex moral questions.

Faculty, therefore, need to distinguish carefully between AI familiarity and AI literacy. Familiarity is relatively easy to acquire. Students experiment with emerging technologies, learn basic prompting techniques, and become comfortable navigating increasingly sophisticated interfaces. Most students will develop some degree of familiarity regardless of what institutions choose to teach.

Literacy is something quite different. Literacy implies disciplined judgment.

Students understand how AI systems influence the production of knowledge. They recognize the strengths and limitations of algorithmic reasoning. They identify circumstances requiring verification, independent judgment, or ethical restraint. They appreciate how AI reshapes professional practice without confusing technological efficiency with disciplinary competence.

Those capacities do not emerge accidentally. They require intentional educational design. This is why Level 4 should not be understood as the inevitable destination of every course.

Upper-division disciplinary courses, professional preparation courses, capstone experiences, graduate seminars, and clinical or field-based learning increasingly prepare students for environments where AI is already integrated into professional practice. Faculty teaching these courses often recognize that graduates who lack the ability to supervise AI responsibly leave the curriculum underprepared for the contexts they will enter.

Business faculty realize strategic decision-making now requires evaluating AI-generated analyses. Nursing faculty recognize that future clinicians must supervise increasingly capable diagnostic systems. Engineering faculty understand that graduates will routinely encounter AI-assisted design environments. Writing faculty discover that authorship itself now includes decisions about when and how AI appropriately participates in the composing process. Theology faculty begin asking how ministers should evaluate AI-generated interpretations while preserving faithful engagement with primary texts and theological tradition.

Notice the common thread. Artificial intelligence will never replace the discipline. It is changing the conditions under which disciplinary expertise is exercised. That distinction is what gives Level 4 its educational coherence.

The learning outcomes remain fundamentally disciplinary. AI literacy becomes embedded within them because competent disciplinary practice increasingly requires sound judgment in AI-mediated environments. Students are not learning AI instead of history, engineering, theology, nursing, or business. They are learning what responsible historical reasoning, engineering judgment, theological interpretation, nursing practice, or business leadership now require in a world where artificial intelligence has become an ordinary feature of professional life.

The curriculum, therefore, evolves without surrendering its intellectual identity. This observation also explains why Level 4 represents such an important developmental threshold.

Earlier levels introduced students to responsible AI use and critical evaluation. Those experiences were valuable, but they remained confined to specific assignments or instructional activities. Level 4 makes a broader institutional claim. AI literacy is no longer incidental to the course. It is now something faculty intentionally promise to teach, assess, and develop.

Once AI literacy becomes an explicit learning outcome, it can no longer depend upon isolated faculty interest or occasional classroom discussion. It must be supported by coherent instructional experiences, meaningful assessment practices, and deliberate curriculum design. Students should encounter repeated opportunities to develop these competencies because the curriculum has declared them essential rather than optional.

This is where AI-CAM begins moving beyond course design toward program design. The question is not whether individual assignments should involve AI, but how graduates should leave the curriculum differently because AI has become part of professional life.

Answering that question requires a level of curricular intentionality that extends beyond individual learning outcomes. If AI literacy is now part of disciplinary competence, students must encounter repeated opportunities to practice it across multiple learning experiences. Artificial intelligence is woven into the course's instructional fabric rather than appearing only in isolated assignments.

What Successful Implementation Looks Like

Successful Level 4 implementation is distinguished by one characteristic above all others: artificial intelligence is no longer treated as an instructional add-on. It is intentionally integrated into the course's educational architecture through clearly articulated learning outcomes. This changes the role AI plays in course design. The central question is whether students have developed measurable competencies for using AI responsibly within the discipline.

That distinction reshapes every aspect of the course.

Assignment design, assessment practices, and instructional activities are no longer organized simply around disciplinary content. They are organized around the relationship between disciplinary expertise and AI literacy. Students continue learning the concepts, methods, and habits of mind that define the field, but with the understanding that competent professional practice increasingly requires the ability to evaluate, supervise, and appropriately integrate artificial intelligence.

The curriculum has become intentionally dual-focused.

Rather than creating isolated "AI assignments," successful Level 4 courses embed AI literacy throughout the semester's learning experiences. Students repeatedly encounter opportunities to make informed judgments about AI within authentic disciplinary work. A business strategy course might require students to document and justify AI-assisted market analyses throughout a semester-long consulting project. A graduate education course may ask future teachers to design classroom activities that intentionally incorporate AI while addressing questions of equity, assessment, and developmental appropriateness. A theology course may require students to evaluate AI-generated interpretations alongside historical and contemporary theological scholarship and explain why certain forms of interpretation remain inadequate despite their apparent fluency.

Notice that the assignments themselves remain disciplinary. AI literacy emerges when students repeatedly practice exercising disciplinary judgment in contemporary conditions, rather than when the technology itself dominates the curriculum.

Once AI literacy becomes an explicit learning outcome, it must be assessed with the same seriousness as every other stated competency. This represents one of the most important differences between Levels 3 and 4. At Level 3, students demonstrate AI evaluation within a particular assignment. At Level 4, AI literacy is expected to develop throughout the course and therefore becomes part of the broader assessment strategy.

Successful assessment does not reward technological enthusiasm. Neither does it reward unnecessary skepticism. Students should receive credit for exercising sound professional judgment. In some situations, that judgment may lead them to appropriately rely on AI.

In others, it may lead them to reject AI-generated recommendations entirely. The educational value lies in the quality of the reasoning supporting those decisions rather than in the decisions themselves.

This emphasis preserves an important distinction. AI literacy is measured less by how effectively students operate artificial intelligence than by how effectively they supervise it.

Disclosure practices continue evolving as well.

By Level 4, transparency has become a normal feature of academic work rather than an isolated requirement attached to particular assignments. Students routinely identify where AI contributed to their work, explain the nature of that contribution, and distinguish clearly between generated content and their own disciplinary reasoning. These disclosures should now resemble the kinds of documentation graduates will increasingly encounter in professional environments. They are concise, informative, and integrated naturally into scholarly practice rather than functioning as separate administrative exercises.

Over time, disclosure becomes less about satisfying institutional policy and more about demonstrating professional accountability.

Students begin recognizing that documenting AI participation protects rather than diminishes their intellectual authority. Clear disclosure allows readers to distinguish technological assistance from human judgment, making the student's evaluative contribution more rather than less visible.

An indicator of successful Level 4 implementation is how students begin to describe their own learning. Earlier levels often produce conversations about AI itself. Students discuss prompting techniques, platform capabilities, or surprising errors generated by different systems. Those conversations remain valuable, but they gradually recede into the background.

Instead, students begin speaking the language of the discipline.

They explain why an AI-generated recommendation failed to satisfy accepted methodological standards. They discuss how disciplinary expertise enabled them to recognize limitations that would otherwise have gone unnoticed. They increasingly understand that artificial intelligence does not diminish the importance of professional knowledge; it heightens it by making expert judgment the indispensable element within environments where artificial intelligence plays an ever-larger role.

Artificial intelligence no longer appears only within selected assignments or isolated learning outcomes. It becomes a recurring intellectual partner throughout the course. Students repeatedly engage AI during drafting, analysis, revision, simulation, design, and reflection while maintaining responsibility for the quality of the final intellectual work.

At that point, the curriculum moves beyond teaching AI literacy toward teaching students how to collaborate responsibly with artificial intelligence across the ordinary rhythms of disciplinary learning.

Where This Level Fails

The strength of Level 4 lies in its curricular clarity. Artificial intelligence is no longer treated as an incidental feature of the learning environment but as an intentional component of disciplinary competence. That clarity, however, also creates new responsibilities. Once AI literacy becomes an explicit learning outcome, institutions can no longer rely upon informal experimentation or individual faculty interest to sustain it. The curriculum has made a promise to students. The educational design must now fulfill that promise.

The most common failure occurs when institutions rewrite learning outcomes without redesigning the curriculum that supports them.

Departments revise course outcomes to include phrases such as "demonstrate AI literacy," "use AI responsibly," or "evaluate AI-generated information." The revised outcomes appear in syllabi, curriculum maps, and accreditation documents. Yet when students move through the course, little has actually changed. The assignments remain the same. Assessment practices remain unchanged. Opportunities to develop the newly articulated competency are limited or inconsistent.

The curriculum has adopted the language of AI literacy without adopting the instructional design necessary to cultivate it. This is what might be called **symbolic integration**. The outcome exists on paper. It does not yet exist within students' educational experience.

Whenever outcomes change, instructional experiences and assessment practices must change with them. Otherwise, the curriculum quietly promises more than it actually delivers.

A second failure emerges when AI literacy becomes detached from the discipline.

One of the defining characteristics of Level 4 is that AI literacy is embedded within disciplinary learning rather than added alongside it. When that integration is lost, faculty often find themselves teaching generic AI skills that could just as easily appear in any campus course.

Students learn prompting strategies. They discuss algorithmic bias. They examine ethical concerns surrounding artificial intelligence. Each of these topics has value. Yet if they remain disconnected from the discipline's intellectual methods, they contribute relatively little to disciplinary education.

- A nursing student should learn AI literacy through clinical reasoning.
- A historian should develop AI literacy through the historical method.
- An engineer should cultivate AI literacy through engineering design.
- Theologians should wrestle with AI through theological interpretation and pastoral judgment.

The distinction matters because universities do not exist primarily to train students in software. They exist to cultivate disciplined ways of thinking. Artificial intelligence should always strengthen that larger educational purpose rather than competing with it.

Another recurring failure appears when faculty confuse exposure with competence.

Because students encounter AI frequently outside the classroom, it is easy to assume that repeated use naturally produces literacy. The evidence suggests otherwise.

Students often grow more comfortable with AI while remaining surprisingly uncertain about when its conclusions deserve confidence. Familiarity creates fluency, but fluency is not the same as judgment. Indeed, one of the paradoxes of AI integration is that confidence frequently grows faster than discernment. Students become more efficient users of increasingly capable systems without becoming equally skilled evaluators of the reasoning those systems produce.

For precisely this reason, Level 4 embeds AI literacy within measurable learning outcomes. Competence must be demonstrated. It cannot simply be assumed, even though students have repeatedly interacted with the technology.

There is also an institutional failure that deserves particular attention.

Departments sometimes adopt Level 4 before the faculty themselves have had sufficient opportunity to develop confidence with AI integration.

Faculty development often proceeds at a different pace than curriculum revision. Instructors suddenly find themselves responsible for teaching and assessing AI literacy without having shared opportunities to discuss disciplinary expectations, assessment standards, or appropriate instructional approaches.

The result is inconsistency. One section of a course may emphasize ethical reasoning. Another focuses primarily on prompting. A third treats AI literacy as little more than responsible citation. Students complete the same course with noticeably different understandings of what the stated learning outcome actually means.

This inconsistency does not reflect faculty indifference. It reflects the reality that curriculum reform requires both faculty development and curriculum revision.

Developmental Transition: Competency Before Collaboration

By embedding AI literacy into measurable learning outcomes, Level 4 acknowledges that responsible engagement with artificial intelligence is now part of competent professional practice across many disciplines. Students are expected not simply to understand AI but to demonstrate disciplined judgment in working with it.

Once those competencies have been established, another developmental possibility emerges. Students are ready to move beyond isolated demonstrations of AI literacy toward sustained collaboration with artificial intelligence across the ordinary rhythms of disciplinary work.

Competence becomes the foundation for collaboration.

That progression introduces Level 5.

Readers interested in seeing this level implemented in an authentic institutional setting may wish to consult **Appendix A**, which presents a detailed case study illustrating how one faculty member redesigned a course using the developmental principles described in this chapter. Rather than serving as a model to be copied directly, the case is intended to demonstrate the reasoning that connects developmental purpose, course design, assessment, and AI integration within a specific educational context.

Chapter 10: Learning Through Structured AI Collaboration - Level 5 - Structured AI Collaboration

Developmental Principle: *Collaboration should follow competence, not replace it.*

Why Choose This Level?

Once students have demonstrated the ability to use artificial intelligence transparently, evaluate it critically, and exercise sound disciplinary judgment, Level 5 addresses the role AI plays in the ordinary practice of learning itself. The movement is from occasional assistance to intentional collaboration.

This transition reflects an important reality about professional life. Graduates entering contemporary workplaces will rarely encounter artificial intelligence in isolation. They will not consult AI once during a project and then set it aside. Increasingly, they will work in environments where AI participates throughout the professional process—during planning, drafting, analysis, revision, simulation, communication, and decision-making. The defining challenge of professional practice is therefore shifting. Success depends less on knowing *whether* to use AI than on learning how to collaborate with it without surrendering professional judgment.

Students arrive at this level having already established three important capacities. They understand how to acknowledge AI transparently. They know where AI appropriately supports learning and where it should not. Most importantly, they have demonstrated the ability to evaluate AI-generated work according to disciplinary standards. Those capacities fundamentally change the nature of the student's relationship with technology.

Artificial intelligence is no longer viewed as either a threat or a convenience. It becomes an intellectual partner whose contributions require continual supervision. That phrase—*intellectual partner*—deserves careful explanation because it is easily misunderstood. Partnership does not imply equality. Neither does it imply shared authority.

Within the AI-CAM framework, collaboration always remains asymmetrical. Artificial intelligence contributes possibilities, alternatives, simulations, drafts, questions, or analyses. The student contributes judgment. AI may expand the range of ideas under consideration, but it does not determine which ideas deserve acceptance. It may accelerate exploration, but it does not establish disciplinary standards. It may generate alternatives, but it cannot assume responsibility for selecting among them.

That responsibility remains human. Indeed, the educational value of Level 5 depends precisely upon preserving that distinction. Meaningful collaboration is never a single interaction. It unfolds through repeated cycles of generation, evaluation, revision, and refinement.

This iterative process closely resembles authentic professional practice. Experienced professionals rarely produce their best work in a single uninterrupted act of individual reasoning. Architects revise designs. Researchers refine hypotheses. Writers reshape arguments. Engineers test and modify solutions. Teachers adapt instructional plans. Ministers reconsider sermons in light of additional reflection. Professional expertise often develops through sustained cycles of generation, evaluation, revision, and refinement.

The emphasis consequently shifts from evaluating isolated AI outputs to supervising an ongoing intellectual process. Faculty no longer ask only whether students recognize AI's limitations. They ask whether students can maintain disciplinary integrity while working alongside increasingly capable technologies over extended periods of inquiry.

Students discover that AI rarely contributes in a consistent manner. One interaction may produce remarkably helpful insights. The next may generate superficial observations or plausible misunderstandings. Productive collaboration, therefore, requires continual discernment rather than occasional verification. Students become responsible for managing the entire relationship between themselves and the technology rather than evaluating isolated moments within it.

This developmental shift also changes the role of reflection.

Earlier levels encouraged students to reflect upon individual instances of AI use. At Level 5, reflection increasingly concerns the collaborative process itself. Students begin recognizing patterns in their interactions with AI. They identify circumstances in which the technology consistently expands their thinking and situations in which it narrows it. They learn where AI stimulates creativity, where it encourages premature closure, and where it quietly reinforces assumptions that deserve greater scrutiny.

These observations become educationally remarkable because they extend beyond artificial intelligence. Students are developing habits of metacognition.

They become increasingly aware of how they themselves think, revise, solve problems, and exercise judgment within complex intellectual environments. Artificial intelligence serves as a catalyst for that awareness, but the developmental outcome remains fundamentally human. Graduates who understand how they reason are better prepared to supervise any future technology than graduates who merely understand today's AI systems.

Students draft, revise, analyze, simulate, compare, and refine their work through ongoing interaction with AI while remaining accountable for every substantive intellectual decision. Faculty no longer observe isolated moments of AI use. They observe students learning how to supervise an evolving collaborative process.

That distinction captures the educational purpose of Level 5. Students are no longer learning primarily *about* AI. Nor are they simply learning *with* AI. They are learning how to exercise mature disciplinary judgment within an ongoing collaborative relationship with increasingly capable technologies.

What Successful Implementation Looks Like

Successful Level 5 implementation is characterized by continuity rather than novelty. Artificial intelligence is no longer introduced through isolated assignments or occasional classroom activities. Instead, it becomes a recurring component of the learning process, appearing whenever it meaningfully advances the course's developmental goals. Students learn to collaborate with AI not because collaboration itself is the objective, but because sustained collaboration provides repeated opportunities to exercise the habits of judgment expected of competent professionals.

In Level 3, students evaluate AI through carefully designed assignments. In Level 4, AI literacy becomes an explicit learning outcome embedded within the curriculum. By Level 5, those competencies are assumed. The course no longer pauses periodically to teach AI literacy because AI literacy has become part of the normal rhythm of learning. Students repeatedly engage with artificial intelligence as they draft, revise, analyze, simulate, and refine disciplinary work. The educational emphasis shifts from learning about responsible AI use, to practicing responsible AI collaboration.

Rather than requiring one major AI activity during the semester, faculty design projects that unfold through multiple stages of interaction. Students may begin by using AI to generate alternative approaches to a complex problem, then compare those alternatives against disciplinary standards, revise their own work in response to new insights, test competing solutions, and reflect upon the reasoning that guided each decision. Artificial intelligence appears repeatedly, but each interaction serves a clearly defined instructional purpose.

At Level 5, Faculty, therefore, design assignments that make the collaborative process visible.

Long-term research projects provide one effective example. Students may use AI throughout the semester to organize literature, identify competing perspectives, challenge emerging arguments, or suggest additional avenues for investigation. Yet each major decision remains subject to disciplinary justification. Students explain why particular AI-generated suggestions were adopted, why others were rejected, and how the final argument reflects their own intellectual responsibility rather than the technology's preferences.

Assessment reflects this developmental emphasis. Students are assessed on the quality of their analyses, interpretations, solutions, or professional decisions. What changes is that the collaborative process itself also becomes evidence of learning. Rather than evaluating only the final product, instructors examine how students exercised judgment throughout the sequence of interactions that produced it.

Assessing that judgment directly, rather than only the disciplinary product it produces, requires a rubric built for the purpose. The one below was designed for project-based work, capstone projects, and other assignments where structured AI collaboration recurs across a semester rather than appearing in a single assignment. It treats prompting strategy, critical evaluation, documentation, and reflective judgment as criteria in their own right, alongside the quality of the professional product itself.

AI Collaboration Quality – Professional Practice (Level 5 / Level 6)

Appropriate for project-based assessments, capstone work, simulation exercises, and professional practice assignments in courses where structured AI collaboration is a recurring course feature. This rubric assesses the quality of collaborative judgment and process documentation alongside professional product quality. Adapt criterion weights to reflect the balance appropriate to your professional context.

Criterion (Weight)	Unsatisfactory – 1	Developing – 2	Proficient – 3	Exemplary – 4
Professional Product Quality (25%)	The professional deliverable (report, analysis, design, or recommendation) is incomplete, inaccurate, or fails to meet the minimum professional standards for the discipline.	The deliverable meets basic professional standards but contains notable gaps in accuracy, completeness, or professional reasoning that would require revision before professional use.	The deliverable meets professional standards for the context. It is accurate, complete, and professionally communicated. It would be defensible in a professional setting with minor revision.	The deliverable exceeds minimum professional standards. It demonstrates sophisticated professional judgment, thorough analysis, and communication quality appropriate for independent professional use.
Prompt Construction & AI Engagement Quality (20%)	Prompts are vague, undifferentiated, or show no evidence of iterative refinement. AI engagement appears passive – the student	Prompts show some specificity but limited strategic development. Some iteration is present, but refinements do not reflect	Prompts are specific, contextually grounded, and show evidence of purposeful iterative refinement. The student's prompt	Prompts are sophisticated, precisely framed, and show clear iterative development from initial inquiry to refined professional application.

	accepted initial outputs without further inquiry.	systematic analytical improvement.	strategy demonstrates developing professional judgment about how to engage AI effectively in this domain.	The prompt sequence itself demonstrates high-level analytical strategy and deep understanding of both the professional domain and the AI tool's capabilities and limitations.
Critical Evaluation & Override Judgment (25%)	AI outputs are accepted without critical evaluation. The student does not demonstrate awareness of AI limitations or make independent judgments about AI-generated content.	Some critical evaluation is present but inconsistent. The student identifies obvious errors but accepts plausible-sounding content without verification or professional judgment.	AI outputs are critically evaluated against professional and disciplinary standards. The student identifies limitations, exercises independent judgment about which AI outputs to use, modify, or reject, and documents their reasoning.	AI outputs are subjected to rigorous, systematic professional evaluation. The student demonstrates expert-level discrimination between reliable and unreliable AI outputs, makes well-reasoned override decisions, and articulates a clear

				professional rationale for each significant AI engagement choice.
Collaboration Documentation & Audit Trail (15%)	Process documentation is absent or so incomplete that the collaboration process cannot be reconstructed. There is no record of how AI contributed to the professional deliverable.	Documentation exists but is incomplete, poorly organized, or inconsistent with the deliverable. It is unclear from the documentation what role AI played in key professional decisions.	Documentation is complete and well-organized. An auditor reviewing the documentation could reconstruct the essential AI collaboration process and understand how AI contributions were evaluated and integrated into the professional deliverable.	Documentation constitutes a professional-grade audit trail. It is precise, thorough, and formatted in a manner consistent with professional practice standards in the discipline. It would withstand client, regulatory, or accreditation review.
Reflective Professional Judgment (15%)	No reflective analysis of the AI collaboration is present. The student	Reflection is present but superficial — general observations about AI's	Reflection demonstrates genuine metacognitive awareness. The student	Reflection demonstrates sophisticated professional self-

	does not demonstrate awareness of how AI shaped the professional deliverable or what that means for professional accountability.	helpfulness or limitations without connection to specific professional decisions or implications.	identifies specific ways AI collaboration shaped their professional thinking, acknowledges limitations and risks, and articulates what independent professional judgment they exercised and why.	awareness. The student situates their AI collaboration experience within the ethical and accountability frameworks of their profession, identifies implications for their own professional development, and articulates a principled approach to AI-assisted professional practice that extends beyond this specific assignment.

Scoring note: Total possible = 4.0 × 5 criteria = 20 raw points. Apply criterion weights as written or redistribute weights to reflect your program's specific emphasis. For professional programs under programmatic accreditation, ensure criterion weighting reflects the professional competency framework in use.

Students are not rewarded for producing elaborate prompts or discovering obscure AI features. Those skills may certainly develop, but they remain secondary. The central concern is whether students exercise increasingly mature judgment while working within an ongoing collaborative relationship. Faculty assess the quality of supervision rather than the sophistication of technological interaction.

Disclosure practices are likewise integrated into the course's normal workflow.

By Level 5, students no longer view AI disclosure as an isolated statement attached to a completed assignment. Instead, documentation becomes part of responsible professional practice. Students maintain concise records of how AI contributed to major stages of a project, identify important moments where human judgment altered the direction of the work, and explain significant decisions affecting the evolution of the final product.

These records need not become exhaustive logs of every interaction. Their educational purpose is not surveillance. Rather, they create opportunities for students to reflect on the collaborative process. Looking back across weeks of work, students often discover patterns that were not obvious while the project was unfolding. They recognize recurring situations in which AI consistently challenges their assumptions, exposes weaknesses in their reasoning, or accelerates routine aspects of the work without improving the quality of the underlying analysis. These observations strengthen metacognitive awareness because students begin to evaluate not only the technology but also their own thinking habits.

Perhaps the clearest indication of successful Level 5 implementation is that artificial intelligence gradually becomes less interesting than the intellectual work surrounding it.

Early in the semester, students often devote considerable attention to AI itself. They discuss its capabilities, compare platforms, and share surprising responses. As the course progresses, however, those conversations begin changing. The technology fades into the background. Students increasingly discuss disciplinary questions, professional judgment, competing interpretations, and the quality of their reasoning. AI remains present, but it no longer dominates attention, having become a normal component of the learning environment rather than an object of fascination.

That realization prepares students for the final developmental transition within AI-CAM.

Once collaboration becomes an ordinary feature of teaching and learning, faculty begin reconsidering the design of the course itself. Rather than asking how students should collaborate with AI on particular projects, instructors begin to ask how artificial intelligence might appropriately support the broader learning environment—through formative feedback, adaptive learning pathways, instructional scaffolding, and other elements of course architecture.

Artificial intelligence moves beyond individual student activity. It becomes part of the educational ecosystem within which learning occurs. The defining achievement of Level 5 is not that students collaborate frequently with AI, but that they retain intellectual authority throughout that collaboration.

Where This Level Fails

Level 5 is perhaps the easiest level within AI-CAM to misunderstand because the language of collaboration can suggest equality where none exists.

Artificial intelligence is not an educational partner. The discipline is. AI is simply one participant within the learning process, and its contributions remain valuable only insofar as they strengthen disciplinary thinking. When that distinction becomes blurred, the developmental purpose of Level 5 begins to unravel.

The most common failure occurs when collaboration gradually becomes dependence.

Unlike the earlier failure at Level 2, where support quietly replaced foundational learning, dependence at Level 5 can emerge unnoticed. Students have already demonstrated disciplinary competence. They are capable of supervising AI responsibly. The problem is that they gradually stop exercising independent judgment because technology becomes the default starting point for every intellectual task.

Instead of framing the problem themselves first, they begin by asking AI. Instead of generating initial hypotheses, they ask AI to suggest possibilities. Instead of drafting an argument before refining it collaboratively, they wait for AI to produce the first version.

Professional collaboration assumes that each participant brings something distinctive to the relationship. The educational purpose of Level 5 is to strengthen the student's disciplinary judgment through repeated interaction with AI. If the student gradually relinquishes responsibility for initiating ideas, framing problems, or exercising independent intellectual curiosity, the collaboration becomes increasingly one-sided. The technology contributes more. The learner contributes less.

A second failure emerges when faculty members mistake repeated use of AI for meaningful collaboration. Frequency is not the same as quality.

I have occasionally encountered courses in which AI appears almost continuously throughout the semester. Students interact with it during nearly every class session and nearly every assignment. Yet the interactions themselves remain remarkably superficial. AI summarizes information, drafts responses, generates discussion questions, and produces revisions, but students spend relatively little time examining why certain contributions prove valuable while others do not.

Students need opportunities to step back from the collaborative process and reflect on what the technology contributed, what it overlooked, and how their own thinking evolved as a result of the interaction. Without these moments of reflection, AI risks becoming educational background noise—constantly present but rarely examined. The collaboration becomes routine. It no longer becomes formative.

Another failure occurs when faculty gradually lower disciplinary expectations because AI appears capable of assisting with increasingly sophisticated work.

This tendency rarely appears intentionally. Instructors often discover that students can complete larger projects, produce more polished writing, and analyze more complex datasets than previous cohorts. These developments are encouraging. Yet they also introduce temptation. Because AI contributes substantially to the work, faculty may begin accepting weaker reasoning, less careful interpretation, or less rigorous disciplinary justification than they would have expected previously.

The assignment grows in scale. The standards quietly shrink.

This represents one of the greatest dangers of advanced AI integration. Artificial intelligence should enable students to engage in more demanding intellectual work, not excuse them from it.

As AI becomes more capable, faculty should expect increasingly sophisticated judgment from students because the technology has removed many routine obstacles to deeper analysis. Higher capability should lead to higher expectations. Not lower ones.

Developmental Transition: Collaboration Before Architecture

Level 5 prepares students for a professional world in which collaboration with artificial intelligence is no longer exceptional but routine. Students learn to supervise AI throughout an extended inquiry process while maintaining responsibility for every intellectual decision.

As collaboration becomes an ordinary feature of learning, attention naturally shifts beyond individual assignments. Faculty begin asking not simply how students should collaborate with AI, but how entire learning environments should be designed to support that collaboration while preserving human judgment and disciplinary integrity.

The focus, therefore, moves from instructional activities to instructional architecture.

That developmental transition defines Level 6.

Readers interested in seeing this level implemented in an authentic institutional setting may wish to consult **Appendix A**, which presents a detailed case study illustrating how one faculty member redesigned a course using the developmental principles described in this chapter. Rather than serving as a model to be copied directly, the case is intended to demonstrate the reasoning that connects developmental purpose, course design, assessment, and AI integration within a specific educational context.

Chapter 11: Designing an AI-Integrated Learning Environment - Level 6 - AI-Integrated Course Architecture

Developmental Principle: *A well-designed course intentionally integrates multiple AI-CAM levels in service of student development*

Introduction

Each level of the AI-Course Application Matrix examined so far has answered the same question: what role should AI play in this particular learning experience? Level 6 asks a different one. Rather than defining a single relationship between students and artificial intelligence, it asks how a faculty member designs an entire course in which several of those relationships operate together, each serving the developmental purpose for which it is best suited.

This is a shift from student development to course design. Levels 0 through 5 describe a continuum that helps faculty decide what relationship students should have with AI as they acquire disciplinary knowledge and professional judgment. Level 6 operates one level up. It treats those relationships not as competing options but as elements of a single architecture, the way a building brings together foundations, classrooms, and laboratories, each constructed differently because each serves a different purpose.

This has been the argument of the book from the start: AI integration should follow educational purpose, not the reverse. Faculty do not begin by asking how AI can be worked into a course. They begin by asking what kind of intellectual formation a given activity requires, and only then decide what role AI should play in it. Level 6 is what happens when those decisions, made consistently across a semester, add up to something coherent.

From Developmental Continuum to Course Architecture

A common misreading of AI-CAM treats it as a ladder that every course should eventually climb toward Level 6. That misreads both the framework and the curriculum. The earlier levels answer a set of situational questions: should this activity be completed independently, should AI serve as disclosed support, should students critique AI output, should AI literacy itself be assessed, should students collaborate with AI as they would in professional practice? None of these questions demands the same answer across an entire course, and the strongest courses rarely give one.

Take an upper-division engineering course. Early in the term, students complete design calculations without AI assistance, so the instructor can see whether foundational analytical skills are actually in place. Level 0, because independent reasoning is the point. Later, students use AI to organize technical literature or summarize relevant standards before developing their own solutions. Level 2, because AI is supporting preparation without doing the engineering. As the course advances, students critique AI-generated design proposals for weaknesses in structural assumptions or code compliance. Level 3, because the AI's output has become an object of disciplinary scrutiny. Course outcomes may require students to demonstrate they can supervise AI-assisted design responsibly. Level 4. The semester might close with a capstone project built through sustained AI collaboration, with students accountable for every consequential decision. Level 5.

Has the course moved through five levels? In a sense. More precisely, the instructor has matched the appropriate relationship between the student and the AI to each stage of learning. AI-CAM is not being climbed here; it is being used as a design vocabulary. Level 6 does not replace the other six levels so much as result from orchestrating them, and the operative question for the instructor is no longer "what level is this course?" but "where in this course does each level serve the students best?"

The Faculty Member as Educational Architect

That question changes the faculty role. Instructors are no longer simply applying an AI policy or designing one assignment at a time; they are designing an environment in which every encounter with AI is placed deliberately. The guiding question becomes: how should this course be structured so that each use of AI serves the intellectual formation the course is meant to produce?

This is architectural thinking in the literal sense. An architect does not start with materials, she starts with purpose, then chooses concrete, steel, or glass according to what a space needs to do. Course design should work the same way. Faculty begin with what students need to know and become, and only then decide where AI belongs and where it should be deliberately absent. That sequencing matters: institutions that ask how AI can improve a course tend to let the technology set the agenda; institutions that ask what the course requires keep AI in its proper, subordinate role.

Faculty working this way are not only delivering content. They are deciding where students should struggle unaided, where support helps without doing the thinking for them, where critical evaluation belongs, where collaboration reflects real professional practice, and where reflection should consolidate what was learned. No single assignment can do all of this; a coherent course is built from activities that each do one of these jobs well.

Designing Learning Environments Rather Than AI Policies

This reframing changes what an institutional conversation about AI can look like. Most such conversations still center on policy: what is permitted, what is prohibited, what the syllabus language should say. Policy work is necessary, but it answers a narrower question than the one that matters. A policy can specify whether a student may use AI on an assignment. It cannot explain why independent work suits one activity and sustained collaboration another, or when students are ready for more demanding forms of AI-assisted inquiry. Those are design decisions, and they are dynamic in a way policy rarely is.

A course built this way does not run on a single AI policy; it runs on a developmental logic that the policy expresses rather than substitutes for. Students come to see that AI is neither uniformly encouraged nor uniformly restricted, but calibrated to what each activity is trying to teach. That consistency matters to students who have otherwise experienced AI rules as a matter of instructor preference, permitted in one classroom, forbidden in the next, with little explanation either way. When the rationale is visible, students stop treating the rule as arbitrary, and faculty gain a stronger basis for explaining their choices than a generic appeal to integrity or workforce readiness.

In practice, this means course planning should start with the developmental map, not the AI policy. Faculty identify where foundational competence needs to be visible, where guided support helps, where critical evaluation should begin, where AI literacy becomes explicit, and where collaboration is warranted, and the policy follows from that map rather than standing in for it.

What This Looks Like in Practice

The strongest Level 6 courses are rarely identifiable by their technology. What distinguishes them is coherence: the relationship between student and AI shifts as the required kind of learning changes, and those transitions feel natural rather than arbitrary. Independent assessment establishes a baseline before collaboration is introduced; AI support is introduced where it strengthens learning without displacing disciplinary reasoning; critical evaluation waits until students know enough to recognize when AI is wrong; collaboration deepens as students show they can supervise it. AI is present throughout, but it is never what the course is about: the discipline is.

That shows up in the rhythm of the course itself. Students might explore a new concept independently, refine their understanding through guided interaction with an AI system designed to ask questions rather than supply answers, bring unresolved problems to class discussion, apply the concept to an authentic disciplinary problem, and reflect on both what they learned and how they came to understand it. Each stage does different work; together, they keep AI in a supporting role rather than letting it become the source of authority in the room. Educational AI used this way should redirect students back to their own reasoning: the value is in the question it raises, not the answer it supplies.

None of this reduces the instructor's need. The sequencing, the disciplinary standards being reinforced, and the judgment calls about what counts as understanding. Those remain the instructor's, whether or not she is present for a given exchange between a student and an AI tool. Regular contact with students still matters: for clarifying confusion an AI system cannot resolve, for modeling the judgment of an experienced practitioner, and for holding students accountable to something more than an automated exchange.

Assessment in such a course draws on more than one kind of evidence, independent work, collaborative inquiry, applied problem-solving, reflective writing, because no single assignment type can show everything the course is trying to develop. Reflection deserves particular attention here, not as a closing formality but as a recurring part of the design: what challenged my assumptions, how has my thinking changed, where did AI genuinely help and where did my own judgment matter more, how will this shape what I do professionally? Questions like these build the habit of examining one's own thinking, arguably a more durable outcome than any single competency the course teaches.

The clearest sign that a course has been designed well is that students eventually stop thinking about the AI at all. Their attention turns to the discipline, the problems, the judgment calls, the standards of the field, while AI continues to do useful work in the background. That invisibility is the point. Good architecture rarely announces itself; it simply lets students notice what they learned and who taught them, rather than what tools were involved along the way.

Characteristics of an Architecturally Designed Course

A few features recur across courses built this way, regardless of discipline or platform.

They are organized around developmental progression, not technological capability. AI shows up where it serves learning and is absent where independent performance is the point, never as a blanket policy applied for its own sake.

They combine several AI-CAM levels within a single course rather than settling on a single level, because no single relationship between student and AI serves every learning objective a course has.

Assessment reflects the same variety: students demonstrate understanding through independent work, collaborative inquiry, applied problems, and reflection, with AI contributing to the process, but human judgment and reasoning remain what is measured.

Reflection recurs throughout the course rather than appearing once at the end, building the kind of self-awareness that enables students to eventually regulate their own learning rather than depend on external structure.

And the faculty member remains the one who sets priorities, defines disciplinary standards, and mentors the development of professional judgment, functions AI can support but not perform.

Taken together, what distinguishes Level 6 is not the sophistication of its tools but the intentionality of its design. AI becomes one element within an environment whose purpose, as always, is the formation of disciplined and competent graduates.

From Course Architecture to Institutional Architecture

The same logic that organizes a single course eventually has to organize an institution, because students experience a curriculum, not a course. A university where individual instructors design architecturally but whose policies, faculty development, and governance remain disconnected has achieved only partial coherence; students encounter thoughtful design in one classroom and contradictory expectations in the next. Extending this architecture beyond the course means asking how faculty are prepared to design this way, how institutional policy reflects developmental thinking rather than technological reaction, how assessment systems recognize disciplinary competence and AI literacy without conflating them, and how governance can encourage innovation without losing sight of institutional mission.

Architecture ultimately exists to connect what students experience one class at a time into an education they experience as a whole.

Seen this way, AI-CAM was never simply a taxonomy of permitted and prohibited uses. It is an architectural framework, and Level 6 is where that becomes visible at the course level. What follows in the chapters ahead applies the same thinking at the institutional level.

Chapter 12: Architectural Patterns Across the Disciplines

The AI-Course Application Matrix is a discipline-neutral framework. Its seven levels do not favor engineering over English, nursing over philosophy, or professional programs over the liberal arts. The developmental logic – from foundational independence to structured collaboration to architectural integration – applies across the curriculum.

Architecture always responds to purpose. Hospitals, libraries, laboratories, and concert halls all embody distinct architectural principles because they serve different forms of human activity. The same is true of curriculum. Every discipline possesses distinctive habits of inquiry, standards of evidence, professional expectations, and developmental priorities. Consequently, AI-CAM cannot produce identical course architectures across every field. The framework remains constant, but its architectural expression varies according to the nature of the discipline.

But the application of that framework is never discipline-neutral. The norms, methods, epistemological assumptions, accreditation requirements, and professional formation goals of each field shape how AI-CAM levels are experienced, which ethical concerns are most pressing, and what AI literacy actually means within a given disciplinary tradition.

This chapter offers brief, structured examples of how AI-CAM integration plays out across distinct fields. Each profile identifies the discipline's default posture toward AI, the most pedagogically appropriate entry-level recommendation, the dominant ethical concerns unique to that field, and a sample learning outcome written to demonstrate what AI literacy looks like when embedded in that discipline's language and standards.

These profiles are not exhaustive treatments. They are orientation documents — designed to help faculty, department chairs, and curriculum committees locate their discipline within the AI-CAM framework and begin the design conversation with shared reference points. Readers are encouraged to adapt, challenge, and extend these profiles based on their own institutional and disciplinary contexts.

Four Questions Every Discipline Must Answer

Every discipline should answer four questions before selecting an AI-CAM level.

1. What foundational competencies require independent performance?
2. What professional AI realities are graduates entering?
3. What ethical obligations are unique to this discipline?
4. Which AI-CAM levels naturally fit the developmental sequence of the curriculum?

Profile 1: Nursing and Health Sciences

Nursing and the allied health disciplines occupy a distinctive position in any conversation about AI integration in higher education. The professional stakes are unusually high: errors in clinical reasoning carry patient safety consequences that no other academic discipline shares in quite the same way. At the same time, AI tools are already deeply embedded in healthcare environments: diagnostic support systems, predictive analytics, medication management tools, and AI-assisted imaging interpretation are routine features of clinical practice in most hospital systems. Graduates who cannot evaluate AI-generated clinical recommendations are professionally underprepared in ways that matter immediately upon licensure.

The default posture in nursing programs has historically leaned toward restriction, driven by the discipline's emphasis on independent clinical judgment and the licensing examination's requirement for demonstrated individual competence. This posture is not misguided; the case for Level 0 in foundational clinical reasoning courses is strong and well-grounded in patient safety concerns. However, treating AI restriction as the default across all nursing coursework misrepresents the professional environment that graduates will enter and fails to develop the evaluative competencies required for safe AI-assisted practice.

The most important ethical concern unique to health sciences is what might be called the *authority transfer problem*: the tendency of clinicians and nursing students to defer to confident algorithmic outputs even when those outputs conflict with clinical observation or professional judgment. AI systems in healthcare are trained on population-level data and cannot account for the individual patient in front of the clinician. Teaching students to maintain evaluative authority over AI tools, to use them as decision support rather than decision replacements, is a patient safety imperative, not merely a general AI literacy goal.

Recommended entry level for foundational clinical courses is Level 0 or Level 1, preserving independent reasoning for licensure-relevant competencies. Upper-division and graduate coursework should move toward Levels 3 and 4, with AI literacy outcomes explicitly tied to clinical decision-making frameworks. Programs with simulation labs may find Level 5 (Structured AI Collaboration) productive in advanced clinical reasoning courses where AI-assisted diagnostic simulations can be debriefed against real clinical scenarios.

At a Glance: Nursing & Health Sciences	
Typical Context	Community colleges, regional comprehensives, and university health science programs

Default Posture	Restrictive in foundational courses; increasingly open in advanced clinical coursework
Entry Level	Level 0–1 for foundational clinical reasoning; Level 3–4 for upper-division and graduate
Key Ethical Focus	Authority transfer: maintaining clinical judgment over algorithmic recommendation
Sample Outcome	Students will evaluate AI-assisted diagnostic recommendations against patient-specific clinical data, identifying conditions under which algorithmic outputs require override or escalation.

Profile 2: Legal Education

Legal education is one of the most consequential contexts for AI integration in higher education. AI tools are already transforming legal practice: contract review, discovery processing, legal research, brief drafting, and predictive analysis of case outcomes are all being performed at scale by AI systems in law firms, corporate legal departments, and public-interest organizations. The American Bar Association has begun issuing guidance on attorney competence obligations regarding AI tools, and several state bars are actively developing formal standards. Law students who graduate without AI literacy will enter a profession that has already moved past them.

The discipline's default posture has been cautious but rapidly evolving. Law schools that maintained blanket restrictions through 2023 have, in many cases, shifted to structured integration by 2025, driven in part by bar association guidance and in part by the recognition that prohibiting tools students will use from day one of practice is an increasingly untenable pedagogical position. The more principled tension in legal education is not about whether to integrate AI but about when independent legal reasoning must be demonstrated without AI assistance, and the answer, as in nursing, is that foundational competency courses have a strong case for Level 0.

The dominant ethical concern in legal education is professional responsibility. The unauthorized practice of law, attorney-client confidentiality, competence obligations, and the risk of AI-generated hallucinations in legal citations are not abstract ethical issues – they are bar discipline matters. Legal education has an unusually direct obligation to embed AI ethics within professional responsibility frameworks rather than treating it as a separate concern. AI literacy in law is inseparable from legal ethics.

The most productive AI-CAM entry point for most law school courses is Level 3, where structured critical evaluation of AI-generated legal analysis against case law and statutory text develops both AI literacy and disciplinary reasoning simultaneously. Clinics and experiential learning courses are natural candidates for Level 5, where AI collaboration in client-facing work can be structured with appropriate supervision and reflection.

At a Glance: Legal Education	
Typical Context	Law schools, pre-law undergraduate programs, paralegal programs
Default Posture	Rapidly shifting from restrictive to structured integration, bar association guidance is accelerating change
Entry Level	Level 0 for foundational legal reasoning; Level 3 as the primary integration point across the curriculum
Key Ethical Focus	Professional responsibility: competence obligations, confidentiality, and AI-generated citation errors

Sample Outcome	Students will identify legally consequential errors in AI-generated case summaries and draft a professional responsibility memo documenting disclosure obligations under applicable bar rules.

Profile 3: Theology and Religious Studies

Theology and religious studies occupy a distinctive position in the AI integration conversation because the discipline's core intellectual commitments, the authority of primary texts, the irreducibility of interpretive tradition, and the formation of moral and spiritual character raise questions about AI that go beyond pedagogical design into questions of meaning, authority, and what it means to know something in a theological sense. AI tools that generate plausible-sounding theological arguments from probabilistic pattern recognition are, from some theological perspectives, not merely methodologically limited but epistemologically confused about the nature of revelation, tradition, and interpretive community.

This does not translate into a blanket argument for restriction. It translates into an argument for unusual deliberateness about what AI can and cannot do in a discipline where the source's authority, the biblical text, the patristic tradition, the magisterium, the confessional standard, is not a matter of data quality but of theological commitment. Students who outsource theological reasoning to AI are not simply taking a shortcut. They are, potentially, forming habits of interpretation that are incompatible with disciplinary standards and, in ministry-preparation contexts, with professional practice.

The primary ethical concern in theological education is what might be called interpretive authenticity, the obligation to engage primary sources directly rather than through AI-generated intermediaries. This concern is not unique to theology (historians face a version of it), but it is particularly acute in programs that understand themselves as forming students for roles in which the personal encounter with sacred texts and traditions is constitutive of the vocation itself.

Faith-based institutions should also attend to the question of institutional identity. AI tools trained on general internet data may generate theological summaries that are technically accurate but theologically thin, or that represent the majority position in a tradition without acknowledging the specific confessional commitments of the institution's tradition. Faculty at confessionally distinctive institutions have good reasons to be more cautious than the general AI-CAM framework requires, and to design Level 1 and Level 2 implementations with particular attention to disclosure of source authority.

At a Glance: Theology & Religious Studies	
Typical Context	Faith-based colleges, seminaries, and universities with religious studies programs
Default Posture	Cautious; concerns about interpretive authority and confessional distinctiveness run deep
Entry Level	Level 1–2 for most coursework; Level 3 productive in apologetics, comparative religion, and ethics courses
Key Ethical Focus	Interpretive authenticity: the obligation to engage primary texts and traditions directly
Sample Outcome	Students will compare an AI-generated summary of a primary theological text with close reading of the original, documenting points of theological distortion and explaining their significance for doctrinal interpretation.

Profile 4: Business and Management

Business education may have the most straightforward case for AI integration of any discipline in higher education, because the professional argument is nearly impossible to contest: AI tools are already standard infrastructure in the environments business graduates enter. Financial modeling, market analysis, strategic planning, operations management, marketing analytics, and human resources functions are all being substantially reshaped by AI systems. An MBA program that does not develop AI literacy is not merely behind; it is failing to prepare its students for professional practice in a specific and measurable way.

The discipline's default posture has shifted faster than almost any other field. Business schools with strong industry advisory boards have received consistent feedback since 2023 that AI fluency is a hiring priority, and that graduates who cannot navigate AI-assisted workflows are at a competitive disadvantage. This has accelerated the adoption of Levels 3 and 4 in business curricula more rapidly than in most other fields, and it has given business faculty a professional-legitimacy argument for AI integration that colleagues in the humanities sometimes lack.

The dominant ethical concerns in business education center on three areas. First, decision accountability: when AI systems contribute to business decisions with measurable organizational, financial, or human consequences, the professional obligation to understand and document AI's role in that decision chain is a governance matter, not merely an academic integrity matter. Second, competitive intelligence ethics: the use of AI tools to aggregate and analyze competitor information raises intellectual property and data ethics questions that business students need to navigate with legal and ethical awareness. Third, workforce impact: business students who will manage organizations need to think carefully about the human consequences of AI-driven efficiency decisions, a dimension of AI literacy that goes well beyond tool proficiency into ethical leadership.

Business programs are strong candidates for Level 4 and Level 5 integration, particularly in strategy, analytics, and capstone courses. The AI Decision Log and professional audit trail approaches described in the Level 4 case study translate naturally into business contexts where process documentation is already a professional norm.

At a Glance: Business & Management	
Typical Context	Business schools, MBA programs, undergraduate business programs
Default Posture	Enthusiastically open; industry pressure for AI fluency is strong and well-articulated
Entry Level	Level 2–3 for introductory courses; Level 4–5 for upper-division and graduate coursework
Key Ethical Focus	Decision accountability: documenting AI's role in consequential organizational decisions
Sample Outcome	Students will develop a documented AI-assisted competitive analysis, including an audit trail of tool use, identification of AI-generated distortions, and a professional memo justifying analytical decisions.

Profile 5: Writing and the Humanities

Writing programs and the humanities disciplines: literature, history, philosophy, cultural studies, have been the site of the most sustained and often the most principled resistance to AI integration in higher education. That resistance is not simply technophobia. It reflects a coherent argument about what humanistic education is for: the cultivation of an individual intellectual voice, the development of close reading and careful argumentation, and the formation of a self capable of making meaning from complex human experience. AI tools that generate fluent prose from statistical patterns are, from this perspective, a direct threat to the core developmental goal of humanistic education.

That argument deserves to be taken seriously rather than dismissed as resistance to change. It is why Level 0 has a strong and defensible place in first-year writing courses and in foundational literature and philosophy courses where independent argumentation is the primary developmental objective. The case for restriction in these contexts is grounded in a defensible theory of what writing instruction is meant to accomplish, not merely a reaction.

At the same time, the humanities face a version of the professional preparation argument that cannot be entirely set aside: graduates who enter journalism, publishing, communications, policy writing, education, and the humanities-adjacent professions will work in environments where AI writing tools are available and, increasingly, expected. A humanities education that produces graduates who can write beautifully but cannot evaluate, supervise, or ethically integrate AI writing tools is incomplete professional preparation, even by the humanities' own standards of critical engagement with the technologies that shape human culture.

The most productive AI-CAM entry point for writing-intensive humanities courses is often Level 3, where students are asked to critique AI-generated arguments, analyses, or interpretations against disciplinary standards, an assignment type that develops both AI literacy and close analytical reading simultaneously. The Level 5 creative writing case study in Chapter 10 illustrates how structured AI collaboration can serve developmental purposes in advanced writing contexts without displacing the cultivation of individual voice.

The dominant ethical concern in writing and the humanities is authorship integrity in the deeper sense of ensuring that students develop and maintain a genuine intellectual voice. AI integration in humanistic disciplines must be designed with unusual care to ensure that the development of that voice is the organizing purpose, and that AI tools serve that purpose rather than substitute for it.

At a Glance: Writing & the Humanities	
Typical Context	Liberal arts colleges, writing programs, humanities departments across institutional types
Default Posture	Mixed to cautious; principled resistance in foundational courses; more openness in advanced contexts
Entry Level	Level 0–1 for foundational writing and close reading; Level 3 productive across upper-division courses
Key Ethical Focus	Authorship integrity: the development and preservation of individual intellectual voice
Sample Outcome	Students will analyze an AI-generated argument for a literary text of their choosing, identify where the AI's interpretation diverges from close textual evidence, and write a counterargument grounded in the primary source.

Profile 6: Engineering and Computer Science

Engineering and computer science are the disciplines in which AI tools have penetrated most deeply and most rapidly. GitHub Copilot and similar code-generation tools are already standard in software development environments. AI-assisted simulation, design optimization, and systems modeling are routine in engineering practice. Computer science students who are not fluent with these tools are behind their peers before they graduate. The professional argument for integration is overwhelming and largely uncontested within the discipline.

The more interesting and contested question in engineering and computer science is not whether to integrate AI but what foundational competencies must be protected from premature outsourcing. The case for Level 0 in introductory programming courses, where students are learning to think algorithmically for the first time, is strong and increasingly well supported by evidence that students who generate working code using AI without understanding its underlying logic struggle in subsequent courses that build on those foundations. The developmental sequencing argument that applies to first-year writing applies with equal force to first-year programming: the tool is available, but using it before the foundational competency is established undermines the formation it is supposed to support.

At more advanced levels, engineering and computer science are natural candidates for Level 5 and Level 6 integration. The structured AI collaboration model in which AI generates initial solutions, students critique and refine them, and the iteration process is documented and assessed, maps directly onto professional software development practices such as code review, pair programming, and iterative testing. Level 6 implementations in computer science courses, where AI tools are embedded in the course's feedback and assessment architecture, are already operational at several research universities and represent some of the most sophisticated AI-CAM implementations currently in practice.

The dominant ethical concerns in engineering involve safety, reliability, and accountability. AI-generated code that is not thoroughly tested can introduce critical vulnerabilities. AI-assisted engineering design that is not validated against physical constraints can produce failures with serious consequences. The ethical obligation to understand, test, and take professional responsibility for AI-generated technical outputs is not merely an academic integrity concern — it is an engineering ethics requirement with professional licensure implications.

At a Glance: Engineering & Computer Science

Typical Context	Research universities, technical institutes, STEM-focused colleges
Default Posture	Open and often enthusiastic; foundational course protection is the primary site of debate
Entry Level	Level 0 for introductory programming; Level 3–4 for intermediate; Level 5–6 for advanced and graduate
Key Ethical Focus	Technical accountability: professional responsibility for testing and validating AI-generated outputs
Sample Outcome	Students will conduct a systematic validation audit of an AI-generated algorithm, documenting test cases, edge conditions, and failure modes, and producing a technical assessment of production readiness.

Profile 7: Education and Teacher Preparation

Teacher preparation programs face a doubled obligation regarding AI integration: they must develop AI literacy in their own students, pre-service teachers, while simultaneously preparing those students to teach in K–12 environments where AI is already present and largely unregulated. The education student who graduates without AI literacy is not only underprepared professionally. She will be responsible for guiding the next generation of students' AI literacy development without a framework for doing so.

This doubled obligation gives education programs an unusual institutional mandate. AI literacy is not merely a professional skill for pre-service teachers – it is a domain of pedagogical content knowledge. Just as teacher candidates learn to teach reading, mathematical reasoning, or scientific inquiry, they need to learn to teach responsible AI engagement. That means educational programs need to integrate AI not only into their course design but also into instructional methods: how do you scaffold AI literacy for a third-grader? How do you design a high school history assignment that develops critical evaluation of AI-generated content? These are the questions education faculty should be building into their programs.

The most important ethical concern in teacher preparation is equity. K-12 AI access is profoundly unequal across schools and districts. Pre-service teachers need to understand that AI literacy instruction is not a neutral technical enrichment – it is a social justice issue in contexts where students from low-income schools have much less access to AI tools, less guidance on their ethical use, and less institutional support for developing the critical evaluation skills that distinguish fluent AI use from dependent AI use. Teachers who emerge from preparation programs with this awareness will design AI-integrated instruction differently from those who treat AI literacy as a technological upgrade available to all students equally.

Education programs are strong candidates for Level 4 integration, with AI literacy explicitly embedded as a learning outcome connected to instructional design competencies. Capstone student teaching seminars may productively operate at Level 5, where candidates engage AI as a collaborative tool for lesson planning, differentiation, and formative assessment design – with structured reflection on what they would and would not use in their own future classrooms.

At a Glance: Education & Teacher Preparation	
Typical Context	Schools of education, colleges with teacher certification programs
Default Posture	Variable; awareness of doubled obligation (personal AI literacy + pedagogical preparation) is growing
Entry Level	Level 2–3 for foundational coursework; Level 4–5 for methods courses and student teaching seminars

Key Ethical Focus	Equity: AI access disparities in K-12 contexts and the social justice dimensions of AI literacy instruction
Sample Outcome	Students will design and critique a K-12 AI-integrated lesson plan, articulating the AI-CAM level of the assignment, the equity considerations addressed in the design, and the assessment strategy for evaluating student AI literacy.

Profile 8: Ministry and Professional Ministry Preparation

Ministry preparation programs present a set of AI integration challenges that are, in some respects, unique and, in others, deeply continuous with those facing all professional formation programs. The goal of formation in ministry education is not merely the transmission of knowledge or the development of competencies. It is the cultivation of a person: one whose intellectual formation, moral character, spiritual depth, and relational capacity are all understood as integral to professional fitness. Any technology that potentially shortcuts that formation process raises questions that go beyond pedagogy into questions of vocation and character.

At the same time, ministers in virtually every tradition already work in environments where AI is present. Sermon preparation tools, pastoral counseling resource platforms, church management systems, and communication tools all incorporate AI features. The minister who has never critically evaluated AI-generated content will be less equipped to supervise these tools wisely in congregational settings than the minister who has learned to engage them with disciplined discernment. Formation for an AI-shaped world is itself a formation goal.

The most significant ethical concerns in ministry preparation involve three related issues. First, pastoral authenticity: congregants who receive AI-generated sermons, AI-drafted pastoral correspondence, or AI-assisted counseling responses without disclosure are receiving something they have not consented to and may not recognize. The obligation of transparency in pastoral relationships is a theological and ethical claim, not merely an academic integrity concern. Second, the formation of prophetic voice: ministry in most traditions requires the capacity to speak with moral authority from a place of genuine conviction and personal encounter with the tradition. AI tools that generate plausible religious language through pattern recognition cannot produce prophetic speech, and formation programs that allow students to substitute AI-generated homiletical content for the hard work of personal theological wrestling are failing their students in vocational preparation. Third, vulnerable populations: pastoral ministry involves frequent contact with people in crisis, grief, or spiritual distress. The use of AI tools in those contexts raises questions about pastoral care standards that transcend the usual framing of AI ethics.

Ministry programs are generally well served by Level 1 and Level 2 integration across most coursework, with careful attention to the boundaries between AI-assisted preparation and AI-substituted formation. Level 3 integration is productive in courses on apologetics, theology of culture, and church and society, where critical evaluation of AI-generated religious content is itself a relevant competency for ministry in contemporary contexts.

At a Glance: Ministry & Professional Ministry Preparation	
Typical Context	Seminaries, Bible colleges, divinity schools, faith-based universities
Default Posture	Cautious to restrictive; concerns about vocational formation and pastoral authenticity are foundational
Entry Level	Level 0–1 for homiletics, pastoral care, and spiritual formation; Level 2–3 for theology and ministry context courses

Key Ethical Focus	Pastoral authenticity: transparency obligations in congregational relationships and the integrity of vocational formation
Sample Outcome	Students will analyze the theological assumptions embedded in an AI-generated sermon outline, evaluate its adequacy for a specified congregational context, and articulate the pastoral and ethical criteria by which a minister should govern AI use in sermon preparation.

Reading Across the Profiles: What the Differences Reveal

Eight profiles across eight disciplines. The variation is real – in default posture, in ethical emphasis, in entry-level recommendation, in the professional stakes that make AI literacy urgent, or in the formation concerns that make restriction defensible. No single template serves all of these contexts, and any institution that attempts to apply a uniform AI policy across its curriculum without regard for these disciplinary differences will produce friction, resistance, and – in the worst cases – policies that protect the wrong things and neglect the right ones.

But the variation also reveals a pattern. Across every profile, without exception, the same three questions turn out to be the decisive ones. First: What foundational competencies must be demonstrated independently, and at what developmental stage? Every discipline has an answer to this, even if that answer differs. Second: What does it mean to exercise professional judgment in an AI-mediated environment in this field, and what does preparation for that judgment require? Third: What are the specific ethical obligations that govern AI use in the professional contexts graduates will enter – and how do those obligations connect to the values the discipline already holds?

These are not new questions. They are the questions that define what it means to educate for a profession rather than merely to train for a role. AI integration does not create them. It makes them newly urgent, newly visible, and newly consequential.

The AI-Course Application Matrix provides the structural vocabulary for answering them at the course and program level. The disciplinary profiles in this chapter provide the contextual specificity that makes structural vocabulary actionable. Together, they give faculty and administrators the tools to move from the question 'What level should this course be?' to the question that actually matters: 'What do our students need to become, and how does AI integration serve – or threaten – that becoming?'

AI-CAM is intentionally discipline-neutral because higher education is not. The framework remains constant. Its educational expression changes because every discipline forms different kinds of thinkers, professionals, and citizens. Good AI integration begins with disciplinary identity.

Part III. From Course Design to Institutional Architecture

Introduction: Building Institutional Capacity

Throughout Part II, the focus of this book has been the individual course.

Each chapter examined a different level of the AI-Course Application Matrix, asking how faculty can make intentional decisions about the role of artificial intelligence within a particular learning environment. We have considered when independent cognitive performance should be protected, when AI may appropriately support learning, when students should begin evaluating AI critically, and how AI literacy can become an explicit component of disciplinary education. The underlying assumption has remained constant throughout: artificial intelligence should be integrated only when it serves learners' developmental needs and the course's educational purposes.

Excellent courses do not spontaneously produce excellent institutions.

A university may house hundreds of thoughtfully designed, AI-integrated classes while still subjecting students to a fragmented, inconsistent, and structurally incoherent educational experience. One instructor may prohibit AI entirely. Another may encourage unrestricted use. A third may require sophisticated AI collaboration without students having first developed the evaluative habits that make such collaboration educationally sound. Each decision may be individually defensible. Collectively, however, they may fail to communicate a coherent educational philosophy.

Because students experience holistic curricula rather than isolated courses, they move continuously along a developmental continuum—from introductory baselines to advanced specialization. Along that journey, they inevitably construct their own understanding of what the institution values. When expectations surrounding artificial intelligence differ dramatically from course to course without any visible educational rationale, students often conclude that AI policies are simply matters of personal preference. What faculty understand as thoughtful disciplinary autonomy can appear to students as institutional inconsistency.

The challenge, therefore, is to help institutions design coherent educational experiences, not merely to help individual faculty design good courses.

Parts I and II have argued that artificial intelligence is fundamentally a curricular question rather than a technological one. Part I established the philosophical foundation through the C.L.E.A.R. framework and introduced AI-CAM as the developmental architecture through which those principles are implemented. Part II translated that architecture into course design, demonstrating how different levels of AI integration become appropriate at different stages of student development.

The next step is to ask what happens when those course-level decisions are viewed together.

- How does an institution create coherence without sacrificing disciplinary diversity?
- How does it encourage innovation while preserving academic freedom?
- How does it prepare faculty for a technological landscape that continues to evolve?
- How does it assure accrediting bodies, governing boards, employers, and students that AI integration reflects intentional educational design rather than isolated experimentation?

These are institutional questions. They cannot be answered solely at the level of individual course design. Just as students develop, institutions do too.

Universities rarely move directly from uncertainty to mature AI integration. They first cultivate faculty understanding. As faculty confidence grows, departments begin developing shared language and common expectations. Institutions gradually establish governance structures, assessment practices, and policies that support rather than constrain thoughtful innovation. Eventually, artificial intelligence becomes neither a disruptive novelty nor a strategic initiative. It becomes one component of a coherent educational architecture that can adapt as technologies continue to evolve.

This developmental progression mirrors AI-CAM's philosophy.

- Growth is intentional.
- Growth is sequential.
- Growth is always directed toward educational purpose rather than technological sophistication.

The institutional application of AI-CAM is not simply the aggregation of many Level 0 through Level 6 courses. AI-CAM was never intended to function only as a course-design framework. Properly implemented, it becomes an institutional architecture that aligns faculty development, curriculum planning, assessment, governance, accreditation, and strategic leadership around a common educational philosophy. Individual courses remain distinct because disciplines remain distinct. Coherence emerges from ensuring that every level expresses the same educational commitments in different developmental forms. In this sense, institutions must learn to think architecturally.

A well-designed campus contains laboratories, libraries, classrooms, performance halls, residence facilities, and places for reflection. Each space serves a different purpose while contributing to a unified educational environment. Curriculum functions in much the same way. Introductory courses preserve foundational learning. Intermediate courses cultivate disciplinary judgment. Advanced courses increasingly resemble professional practice. AI integration should exhibit the same coherence. Different courses occupy different places along the AI-CAM continuum because they serve different educational purposes within the student's broader developmental journey.

Institutional leadership is exercised through stewardship.

Stewardship creates the conditions for thoughtful educational decisions to flourish. It provides faculty with a shared vocabulary, meaningful professional development, coherent policies, and assessment practices that reinforce, rather than undermine, the educational purpose. It protects academic freedom while making institutional commitments visible. It allows innovation to emerge from disciplined inquiry rather than technological enthusiasm.

The chapters that follow examine that work of stewardship from four complementary perspectives.

Chapter 13 considers the development of institutional capacity through faculty learning and professional formation. Institutions cannot implement thoughtful AI integration unless faculty possess the educational judgment required to design it.

Chapter 14 turns to institutional coherence, exploring how governance, policy, and organizational structures can support rather than constrain responsible innovation.

Chapter 15 addresses institutional quality, examining how assessment, documentation, and accreditation demonstrate that AI integration remains aligned with educational mission and measurable student learning.

Finally, Chapter 16 considers institutional responsibility over time. The challenge facing higher education is not simply to respond wisely to today's artificial intelligence systems, but to develop institutions capable of responding wisely to technologies yet to be invented.

The enduring question is whether higher education will continue to react to technological change one innovation at a time, or whether institutions will develop the educational wisdom, organizational capacity, and architectural coherence necessary to remain faithful to their mission regardless of how technology evolves.

The chapters in this part argue that institutional maturity is not measured by the amount of artificial intelligence present across the curriculum. It is measured by the quality of educational judgment through which institutions decide where artificial intelligence belongs—and where it does not.

That is the work of institutional architecture. And it is the necessary bridge between designing excellent courses and building universities prepared to educate thoughtfully in an AI-mediated world.

Chapter 13. Developing Institutional Capacity

Faculty Formation for AI-CAM Implementation

From Faculty Development to Institutional Learning

Faculty development occupies an unusual place in contemporary conversations about artificial intelligence in higher education.

Nearly every institutional report identifies it as essential. Strategic plans routinely acknowledge that faculty preparation will determine the success or failure of AI integration. Administrators consistently recognize that policy alone cannot reshape teaching, and faculty themselves frequently identify professional development as one of the institution's greatest needs. Yet faculty development often enters the conversation surprisingly late.

Institutions commonly begin by evaluating AI platforms, drafting policy statements, revising academic integrity procedures, or selecting institutionally approved technologies. These are important decisions. None addresses the central educational question.

Throughout this volume, I have argued that AI integration is fundamentally a curricular architecture decision rather than a technological one. That principle applies just as fully at the institutional level. Universities do not become AI-integrated by adopting new software. They become AI-integrated because faculty gradually develop new ways of thinking about learning outcomes, assessment, authorship, intellectual formation, and the appropriate role of artificial intelligence within each discipline.

Faculty development is the process through which institutions learn. While software training assumes a predetermined technical destination, true institutional learning requires collective discernment to determine how generative systems intersect with the enduring metrics of higher education. Faculty are implementing established practices and engaging in the careful educational work of exploring how emerging technologies intersect with the enduring purposes of higher education.

Universities remain responsible for cultivating intellectual judgment, ethical reasoning, disciplinary competence, and professional formation. Artificial intelligence introduces new conditions for exercising those responsibilities, but it does not replace them. Faculty, therefore, require something deeper than operational familiarity with emerging technologies. They require opportunities to reconsider how those enduring educational responsibilities should be expressed within increasingly AI-mediated learning environments.

The Developmental Challenge Facing Institutions

Every institution currently navigates an uneven educational landscape.

Students increasingly arrive having already encountered artificial intelligence in meaningful ways. Some have incorporated generative AI into writing, programming, research preparation, or study habits long before entering the university. Others possess only limited experience but nonetheless recognize AI as an ordinary feature of the digital environments they inhabit. Regardless of individual experience, few students now regard artificial intelligence as a distant possibility. For many, it is simply part of everyday academic life.

Faculty often occupy a much wider range of positions. Some have become early innovators. They redesign assignments, experiment with new assessment approaches, and continually evaluate the educational possibilities of emerging AI systems. Others remain curious but cautious. They recognize AI's significance while continuing to ask thoughtful questions about where it appropriately belongs within their own disciplines.

Still others remain deeply skeptical. Their reservations are not necessarily directed toward the technology itself. More often, they concern the educational consequences that accompany it. They question whether AI strengthens learning or merely improves performance. They wonder whether foundational competencies can develop when powerful generative systems take on an increasing share of academic work. They ask whether assessment continues to measure learning or merely the effective use of increasingly sophisticated technologies.

These differences should not surprise us. Diversity of perspective has always been one of higher education's greatest strengths. Artificial intelligence has not altered that reality. If anything, it has made it more visible.

The institutional challenge, therefore, is not persuading every faculty member to reach identical conclusions about artificial intelligence. It is cultivating sufficient shared educational understanding that faculty across disciplines can make thoughtful, coherent, and pedagogically defensible decisions while preserving the disciplinary autonomy upon which universities depend.

That objective requires considerably more than technology training. It requires institutional learning.

Understanding Faculty Hesitation

Faculty often express concerns about artificial intelligence because they take teaching seriously. Some worry that premature AI integration may interfere with the development of foundational disciplinary competencies. Others question whether current assessment practices can still provide reliable evidence of student learning when authorship becomes increasingly difficult to interpret. Some raise ethical concerns regarding privacy, intellectual property, algorithmic bias, or institutional responsibility. Others acknowledge a far more practical reality.

Meaningful course redesign requires substantial time.

Faculty balancing teaching, scholarship, advising, committee responsibilities, accreditation work, mentoring, and institutional service understandably approach any major curricular initiative with careful deliberation. Introducing AI thoughtfully into existing courses requires considerably more than adding a policy statement to the syllabus. It often requires reconsidering learning outcomes, redesigning assignments, revising rubrics, and rethinking the relationship between independent performance and technological support.

I have argued that AI integration begins with asking educational questions rather than technological ones. Faculty hesitation frequently represents that very process. The task of institutional leadership is to cultivate an environment in which legitimate educational concerns can be carefully examined, misconceptions can be honestly addressed, emerging evidence can be critically evaluated, and thoughtful instructional judgment can mature over time.

This changes the character of faculty development. Faculty are no longer viewed as reluctant technology users waiting to receive additional instruction. They become educational partners engaged in the difficult work of determining how new technologies should serve the longstanding purposes of higher education.

That posture changes the conversation. Trust gradually replaces defensiveness. Curiosity replaces anxiety. Shared inquiry replaces institutional polarization. These are not merely interpersonal improvements. They are the conditions under which meaningful institutional learning becomes possible.

Faculty Development as Institutional Learning

Once faculty development is understood in this way, another observation follows naturally.

Successful educational innovation has rarely spread because information has become widely available. It has spread because communities gradually developed shared confidence in new educational practices. Individual experimentation eventually became departmental conversation. Departmental conversation gradually informed institutional expectations. Over time, isolated innovations became common educational practice—not because uniformity was imposed, but because collective professional judgment matured.

Artificial intelligence appears to follow the same developmental pattern. This suggests that faculty development should be designed differently from how many institutions presently imagine it. Rather than asking, How do we train faculty to use artificial intelligence?, institutions may find greater educational clarity by asking a different question:

How do we help faculty develop the professional judgment necessary to determine when artificial intelligence strengthens learning, when it weakens learning, and when it should remain absent altogether?

That question is entirely consistent with the developmental philosophy underlying the AI-Course Application Matrix.

Throughout Part II, AI-CAM described the progressive development of students as they moved from independent performance toward increasingly sophisticated forms of AI-supported professional judgment. Institutions undergo a remarkably similar progression. Early efforts emphasize awareness and experimentation. As faculty confidence grows, instructional practices become more intentional. Departments begin developing a common language. Course redesign becomes more coherent. Eventually, institutions acquire the collective capacity to integrate future technologies without continually starting from scratch.

Faculty development, therefore, mirrors the developmental architecture that AI-CAM describes for students. Understanding that progression provides the foundation for everything that follows.

The remainder of this chapter examines how institutions cultivate that maturity through the progressive development of faculty competencies, the creation of sustainable pathways for professional growth, the building of collaborative instructional communities, and, ultimately, the establishment of a culture in which responsible AI integration becomes an ordinary expression of thoughtful curriculum design rather than an extraordinary response to technological change.

Developing Faculty Capacity

Early conversations surrounding artificial intelligence in higher education often focused on operational competence. Workshops introduced faculty to emerging AI platforms, demonstrated prompt construction, generated sample assignments, and illustrated the capabilities of increasingly sophisticated language models. Such experiences served an important purpose. They reduced uncertainty, increased familiarity, and enabled faculty to experiment with technologies they had previously encountered only through media reports or student conversations.

Yet familiarity should not be mistaken for readiness. Knowing how to produce an AI-generated outline is not the same as knowing whether such an activity strengthens learning within a particular course. Understanding how a chatbot produces feedback does not determine whether that feedback should be incorporated into assessment practice. Learning to generate text efficiently says remarkably little about how curriculum ought to be redesigned in response.

Operational knowledge answers technological questions. Faculty development must prepare educators to answer educational questions.

Institutions should resist measuring faculty preparedness by the number of AI tools instructors can operate. A more meaningful question is whether faculty possess the educational judgment necessary to determine where artificial intelligence contributes to intellectual formation and where it threatens it. That distinction transforms faculty development from software training into professional formation. The goal is not faculty who are AI specialists. The goal is faculty who are increasingly thoughtful architects of learning environments.

Five Domains of Faculty Capacity

Responsible AI integration depends upon growth in five interconnected areas. Together, they represent a developmental framework for faculty learning rather than a checklist of isolated competencies.

1. Understanding Artificial Intelligence as an Educational Technology

Faculty need not become computer scientists in order to teach effectively with artificial intelligence.

They do, however, require sufficient conceptual understanding to evaluate AI critically rather than treating it as either magical or mysterious. This understanding begins with relatively straightforward questions.

- How do large language models generate responses?
- Why do hallucinations occur?
- What kinds of reasoning do these systems perform well?
- Where do they consistently struggle?
- Why do confidently expressed answers sometimes prove unreliable?

Faculty who understand these underlying characteristics are better positioned to design appropriate learning experiences because they recognize that AI systems produce probabilistic language rather than verified disciplinary knowledge. They understand why verification remains essential, why disciplinary expertise cannot be delegated to technology, and why students require guidance in critically evaluating AI outputs.

Artificial intelligence becomes neither an educational miracle nor an existential threat. It becomes another instructional technology whose value depends entirely upon how thoughtfully it is integrated into learning.

2. Designing Learning Rather Than Adding Technology

Historically, instructional technologies have entered the academy through additive inflation rather than structural redesign. Faculty routinely layer discussion boards, recorded lectures, or real-time polling software onto legacy syllabi without auditing the underlying course architecture. Artificial intelligence initially invites a similar response. Faculty ask where AI might fit within an existing assignment.

The more important question is whether the assignment still reflects the course's developmental purpose, a concern that recurs throughout the AI-CAM framework.

Technology should never be inserted into the curriculum merely because it is available. Its educational value depends upon whether it strengthens constructive alignment among learning outcomes, instructional activities, and assessment.

Faculty, therefore, require the capacity to redesign learning rather than simply augment it. The question guiding course redesign, therefore, becomes remarkably consistent. What kind of thinking is this course trying to develop?

Once that question has been answered clearly, AI integration decisions become considerably easier.

3. Preserving Ethical Judgment

Every technological innovation introduces new ethical questions. Artificial intelligence introduces unusually visible ones. Questions surrounding authorship, transparency, intellectual property, privacy, bias, accessibility, environmental stewardship, and professional responsibility now intersect directly with everyday teaching.

Faculty development must therefore extend beyond institutional compliance. Ethical judgment is not merely the ability to explain institutional policy. It is the ability to reason carefully through situations where policy alone provides insufficient guidance.

- Should students disclose AI-supported brainstorming?
- When does editing become authorship?
- How should instructors respond when AI-generated work demonstrates genuine understanding?
- What obligations do faculty have regarding student privacy when third-party AI systems are introduced into coursework?

Questions such as these rarely yield simple procedural answers. They require thoughtful professional judgment grounded in disciplinary standards, institutional values, and educational purpose. Faculty development should therefore cultivate ethical reasoning rather than merely communicating rules.

Throughout earlier chapters, C.L.E.A.R. has provided the philosophical foundation for this work. Faculty first learn the educational commitments represented by Critical Thinking, Learning Outcomes, Ethical Use, Alignment, and Reflection. AI-CAM then provides the developmental architecture through which those commitments become visible within actual courses.

The relationship remains the same here. Educational philosophy precedes technological implementation.

4. Rethinking Assessment

Perhaps no dimension of faculty development proves more demanding than assessment.

Artificial intelligence has not merely introduced new instructional possibilities. It has challenged long-standing assumptions about what assessment measures.

Traditional assessment frequently assumed that finished academic products represented independent intellectual performance. Increasingly, faculty recognize that finished products reveal considerably less about learning than they once did.

Students may now receive meaningful assistance with brainstorming, drafting, revising, organizing, coding, or data analysis. The educational question, therefore, changes. Faculty no longer ask only whether students produced quality work. They ask whether students exercised sound judgment throughout the process that produced it.

Within an AI-integrated course, the value of automated feedback therefore depends not simply on its speed or accuracy but on whether students evaluate it, act upon it, and demonstrate how it influenced subsequent work.

This shift requires new assessment habits. Faculty learn to distinguish disciplinary mastery from AI literacy. They evaluate intellectual contribution alongside technological assistance. They examine both process and product. They increasingly assess reasoning, verification, reflection, and professional judgment rather than relying exclusively upon polished final submissions.

AI-assisted feedback should be designed as a cycle that produces student action rather than as a more efficient means of delivering comments. Boud and Dawson (2023) locate effective feedback at program, course, and individual-assignment levels and identify timing, sequencing, dialogue, student self-assessment, and evidence of feedback use as important elements of feedback-literate teaching.

Such changes initially appear substantial. Over time, they become natural extensions of educational purpose. Assessment once again aligns with the developmental architecture of learning rather than with assumptions inherited from earlier technological contexts.

5. Reclaiming the Faculty Role

One of the more curious assumptions surrounding artificial intelligence is that increasingly capable technologies necessarily reduce the importance of faculty. Experience consistently suggests the opposite.

As routine instructional activities come to depend more on AI, the uniquely human dimensions of teaching become more visible. Students continue needing guidance in interpreting complex ideas. They require encouragement when learning becomes difficult. They seek clarification when competing interpretations emerge. They benefit from instructors who can connect disciplinary knowledge with ethical reflection, professional judgment, and personal intellectual growth.

The responsibilities to cultivate understanding, interpret meaning, and develop people become increasingly central as AI assumes greater responsibility for routine instructional support. Faculty development should therefore strengthen rather than diminish professional identity.

Institutions are not preparing instructors to compete with artificial intelligence. They are preparing them to exercise those educational responsibilities that technology cannot meaningfully assume.

Building Institutional Capacity

Faculty development has traditionally been understood as an individual undertaking. Faculty attend workshops, read new scholarship, redesign assignments, and experiment with unfamiliar instructional approaches. These activities remain important, but they are insufficient to produce lasting institutional change.

Teaching has always possessed a deeply personal dimension. Every instructor develops individual habits, preferences, disciplinary emphases, and pedagogical philosophies. Artificial intelligence does not eliminate that individuality, nor should it. Yet AI integration introduces questions that extend beyond the boundaries of any single classroom. Students move continually from course to course, department to department, and program to program. Their educational experience is shaped not only by excellent individual instructors but by the coherence—or incoherence—of the institution as a whole.

Faculty development, therefore, cannot remain solely an individual enterprise. It must gradually become a shared institutional practice. The shift from individual to institutional learning mirrors the developmental progression outlined throughout this book.

Students learn first as individuals before becoming members of professional communities. Faculty similarly develop individual competence before contributing to institutional capacity. Only then does an institution begin acquiring what might properly be called educational maturity.

Communities of Practice

Educational innovation rarely spreads when a single faculty member discovers an effective instructional strategy. It spreads because faculty begin talking with one another.

Throughout higher education, some of the most significant instructional advances have emerged not through formal mandates but through informal professional conversations. Faculty observe one another's teaching, compare assessment practices, discuss classroom successes and failures, and gradually refine their collective understanding of what effective instruction requires.

Artificial intelligence should be introduced into institutions through this same process. Communities of practice provide the natural environment within which AI integration matures. Within these communities, faculty do considerably more than exchange technological advice. They compare educational reasoning.

One instructor explains why Level 0 remains essential within introductory laboratory work. Another describes how structured AI evaluation transformed a senior seminar. A colleague from another discipline raises ethical concerns that had not previously been considered. An instructional designer demonstrates how revised assessment strategies strengthened alignment between learning outcomes and AI use.

None of these conversations produces immediate institutional uniformity. That is not their purpose. Instead, they cultivate something more valuable. Shared educational vocabulary. Over time, faculty begin to ask similar questions, even when their answers differ.

- What developmental purpose does this assignment serve?
- What role should AI play at this stage of learning?
- How should assessment reveal authentic intellectual growth?
- Where should independent performance remain protected?

Notice that these questions are not technological. They are educational. Communities of practice, therefore, accomplish something that formal workshops often cannot; they normalize thoughtful professional conversation about curriculum. Artificial intelligence is gradually becoming another subject of educational inquiry rather than a disruptive technological exception.

That transition marks an important stage of institutional learning.

The Expanding Role of Instructional Designers

As faculty conversations become more sophisticated, another professional role becomes correspondingly important. Instructional designers. Artificial intelligence has expanded the responsibilities of instructional design.

Historically, instructional designers often focused on learning management systems, online course organization, accessibility, instructional technologies, and constructive alignment. Those responsibilities remain central. AI integration, however, places instructional designers at an important intersection within institutional life.

Faculty bring disciplinary expertise. Administrators bring institutional priorities. Technology specialists bring technical knowledge. Instructional designers translate among them. They help faculty move from educational philosophy to instructional architecture.

Throughout this volume, the relationship between C.L.E.A.R. and AI-CAM has remained consistent.

- C.L.E.A.R. defines the educational commitments.
- AI-CAM operationalizes those commitments through curriculum design.

Instructional designers increasingly help faculty make that translation visible within actual courses. This role extends well beyond technical support. Instructional designers occupy the space where these questions become practical design decisions. Their contribution is therefore architectural rather than technological. They help institutions preserve educational coherence while allowing considerable disciplinary diversity.

That balance becomes increasingly valuable as AI integration expands across departments.

A Developmental Pathway for Institutions

The progression described throughout this chapter can now be viewed at the institutional level. Institutions rarely move directly from initial awareness to comprehensive AI integration. They mature gradually.

Initially, faculty become aware of emerging technologies and begin exploring their educational implications. As confidence grows, carefully designed experimentation becomes possible. Individual courses are redesigned. Early successes and failures provide valuable institutional learning. Departments then begin examining AI integration collectively. Shared language develops. Faculty compare approaches. Coherence gradually replaces isolated experimentation.

Eventually, institutions begin thinking architecturally. Faculty development, instructional design, assessment, governance, and curriculum planning increasingly operate within a common educational framework.

Faculty development alone cannot sustain institutional coherence indefinitely. As faculty capacity expands, institutions must begin to ask how educational commitments should be expressed consistently across policy, governance, accreditation, and organizational structures.

Chapter 14: Building Institutional Coherence

Policy, Governance, and AI-CAM Alignment

Institutional policy is the architecture that either enables or undermines everything else in this book. A faculty member can design an exemplary Level 4 course with well-calibrated AI literacy outcomes, a thoughtfully constructed hybrid authorship rubric, and a rigorous process documentation system — and still find that work undermined if the institution's academic integrity policy treats all AI use as a violation, if the syllabus template provides no space for AI-CAM level designation, or if the registrar's system has no mechanism for tracking AI integration across program curricula. Policy coherence is a precondition for good course design, not a luxury that follows from it.

The breadth of institutional responsibility is reflected in Sposato's (2025) taxonomy of AI in educational leadership, which encompasses teaching and learning, administrative efficiency, decision support, student services, strategic planning, governance and compliance, ethical leadership, and diversity, equity, and inclusion. This range confirms that institutional AI integration cannot be assigned to a single office or treated solely as an information-technology initiative.

Chapter 3 established that ethical responsibility extends beyond the individual classroom as AI becomes more deeply integrated into learning. Privacy, equity, accountability, and coherent expectations eventually require institutional responses that individual faculty members cannot provide alone. This chapter takes up that responsibility at the institutional level, asking how ethical commitments become durable structures of policy, governance, risk management, and accountability.

Yet policy coherence in AI integration remains the exception rather than the rule. Bian et al. (2024), citing a UNESCO survey of more than 450 educational institutions, report that only 13 percent of universities had established guidance on generative AI. Across the institutions that had guidance, only 40 percent provided it through written policies, while nearly 20 percent of respondents were uncertain whether their institutions had any guidance at all. These findings point not only to a shortage of institutional policies but also to the incomplete and inconsistent character of much existing guidance.

This chapter develops a comprehensive framework for AI governance in higher education, organized around four interconnected responsibilities: academic policy harmonization, risk management, accreditation accountability, and interdepartmental coordination. Each section addresses both the practical design questions facing institutions and the durable structural principles that should guide policy development regardless of how the specific regulatory and technological landscape evolves. Throughout, the AI-Course Application Matrix (AI-CAM) is treated not merely as a pedagogical tool but as an institutional governance instrument—a shared vocabulary that enables policy coherence across departments, disciplines, and administrative units.

A Note on Accreditation Standards and Currency

This chapter addresses accreditation governance at the level of durable structural expectations — the kinds of evidence, documentation, and accountability that accrediting bodies have consistently required across decades and revisions of standards. Specific criterion numbers, policy language, and compliance thresholds change more rapidly than a book can track. Readers should verify current standards with their specific regional or programmatic accreditor before developing institutional AI policy documentation. The structural principles articulated here are designed to remain applicable regardless of the specific standards in effect at the time of implementation.

Academic Policy Harmonization

Bian et al. (2024) identify institutional inertia, cultural apprehension, insufficient professional development, and unclear institutional policies as significant barriers to faculty adoption of AI. Policy coherence must therefore be accompanied by sustained capacity building rather than treated as a substitute for it.

The first governance challenge facing most institutions is the fragmentation of existing policies that bear on AI use, yet were not designed with AI in mind. Academic integrity policies, intellectual property policies, student data privacy policies, and assessment policies all intersect with AI integration, often creating contradictions, ambiguities, or gaps that leave faculty without clear guidance and students without consistent expectations.

Academic integrity policy is the most immediate site of conflict. Policies written before the widespread availability of generative AI tools typically define academic dishonesty in terms of plagiarism. Generative outputs fundamentally elude legacy definitions of plagiarism: they represent neither another individual's intellectual property nor traditionally copyrighted material. Institutions that apply plagiarism frameworks to AI use produce enforcement inconsistencies because the underlying conceptual framework does not match the actual integrity concern (Perkins et al., 2023).

The appropriate response is not to abandon academic integrity policy but to modernize it. Institutions should articulate AI integrity as a distinct concept, *cognitive authenticity*, that sits alongside but is not reducible to traditional plagiarism. Cognitive authenticity, as developed throughout this volume, refers to the obligation to represent one's intellectual contribution accurately: to disclose AI assistance transparently, to exercise genuine evaluative judgment over AI-generated content, and to preserve independent cognitive performance where course design requires it. This framing is both more accurate and more actionable than the language of plagiarism applied to AI contexts.

Syllabus policy is a second harmonization that institutions frequently overlook. Most institutions have syllabus templates and requirements that predate AI integration and provide no structure for communicating AI-CAM level designations, AI disclosure expectations, or AI tool requirements to students. Updating syllabus templates to include a standardized AI Integration Policy section, with a field for AI-CAM level designation and a field for tool-specific permissions and requirements, accomplishes several governance goals simultaneously: it normalizes AI-CAM as institutional vocabulary, it creates a documentation trail that supports accreditation review, it ensures students receive consistent information across courses, and it signals that AI integration is an institutional priority rather than an individual faculty experiment.

Academic Policy Harmonization: Minimum Institutional Actions

1. Reframe academic integrity policy to define 'cognitive authenticity' as a distinct concept alongside traditional plagiarism – with AI-specific disclosure standards and enforcement criteria.

2. Issue IP policy clarification addressing ownership of AI-assisted student work and data privacy obligations when submitting institutional work to third-party AI platforms.

3. Update syllabus templates to include a standardized AI Integration Policy section with fields for AI-CAM level designation, tool permissions, and disclosure requirements.

4. Establish a disclosure citation standard – at a minimum, a departmental template – so that AI attribution is consistent and auditable across courses.

Risk Management Frameworks

Institutional risk in AI integration spans four domains: data security and student privacy; algorithmic bias and assessment fairness; faculty governance and academic authority; and reputational risk from both over-restriction and under-governance. Each domain requires specific institutional responses, and together they constitute a risk management framework that should be developed proactively rather than assembled in response to incidents.

Data Security and Student Privacy

The most immediate legal risk in AI integration involves student data. When students submit academic work to third-party AI platforms, for feedback, for generation, for evaluation, that work may be used by the platform to train future models, stored on servers outside institutional control, or shared with third parties under terms of service that students and faculty have not carefully read. Under the Family Educational Rights and Privacy Act (FERPA), institutions are responsible for ensuring that students' educational records are not disclosed to third parties without appropriate consent or authority.

Institutions managing this risk should establish a tiered AI tool approval process: a category of institutionally approved tools that have been vetted for FERPA compliance and data privacy standards; a category of permitted-with-disclosure tools that faculty may use with appropriate student notification; and a category of prohibited tools where data handling practices are incompatible with institutional privacy obligations. This tiered structure provides faculty with meaningful flexibility while ensuring compliance with institutional obligations. It also provides the documentation trail that accreditors expect when reviewing institutional data governance practices.

Algorithmic Bias and Assessment Fairness

As AI tools become embedded in feedback, formative assessment, and adaptive learning systems at higher AI-CAM levels, algorithmic bias may produce systematically different results across identifiable student groups, creating significant equity and governance concerns (Baker & Hawn, 2022). Title VI of the Civil Rights Act of 1964 prohibits intentional discrimination based on race, color, or national origin in programs receiving federal financial assistance. An institution's use of an AI system does not remove that obligation: when AI-informed policies or decisions treat similarly situated students differently based on a protected characteristic, Title VI concerns may arise (42 U.S.C. § 2000d). Institutions should therefore examine AI systems for differential performance and discriminatory treatment, while recognizing that unequal statistical outcomes alone do not necessarily establish a Title VI violation.

Institutional risk management in this domain requires that AI tools used in assessment or feedback contexts undergo periodic bias audits: structured reviews of tool outputs disaggregated by student demographic characteristics. Faculty who observe patterns suggesting that AI feedback tools systematically rate certain student populations lower should have a clear reporting pathway that triggers an institutional review. And AI tools used in any summative assessment capacity, tools whose outputs directly influence grades, should require explicit faculty review and override authority, not merely nominal faculty approval of AI-generated scores.

Faculty Governance and Academic Authority

A risk that institutions frequently underestimate is the governance risk created when AI integration outpaces faculty deliberation. When administrators adopt AI platforms for instructional use, when curriculum committees approve AI-integrated courses without faculty-wide discussion of standards, or when institutional AI policies are developed by IT or legal offices without faculty governance input, the resulting policies lack the legitimacy that faculty adoption requires, as most accreditation bodies state.

Effective AI governance in higher education places faculty deliberative bodies — curriculum committees, academic senates, faculty councils — at the center of policy development rather than at the end, as ratifiers of administrative decisions. This is not merely a political calculation. It is an educational one: faculty who participate in developing AI integration standards understand them more deeply, implement them more consistently, and model for their students the principled deliberation about AI tools they are charged with developing.

Accreditation, Accountability, and AI-Integrated Documentation

Accreditation is the mechanism through which higher education institutions demonstrate to external reviewers that their educational programs meet established standards of quality, integrity, and continuous improvement. AI integration does not change these expectations. It creates new documentation obligations within them.

The five structural expectations that AI-integrated governance must address, across all accrediting bodies regardless of the specific standards language in effect at any given time, are student learning outcomes, academic integrity, faculty authority, institutional effectiveness, and continuous improvement. Each maps directly onto dimensions of the AI-CAM framework that, if properly documented, provide accreditors with the evidence they need to assess institutional compliance.

Durable Accreditor Expectation	AI-CAM Documentation That Addresses It
Student learning outcomes are clearly defined, measurable, and assessed	AI-CAM level designations in syllabi; alignment maps showing how AI literacy outcomes connect to program goals; rubrics with explicit AI literacy criteria at Levels 3–6
Academic integrity is actively maintained, and students understand expectations	Standardized AI disclosure requirements; cognitive authenticity policy; AI-CAM level communication in syllabi; faculty training records on AI integrity standards
Faculty retain authority over curriculum, instruction, and assessment	Documentation that faculty – not AI systems – make all final grade determinations; governance records showing faculty deliberation in AI policy development; Level 6 oversight protocols

Institutional effectiveness is monitored through systematic data collection	AI-integrated course outcome data disaggregated by student population; bias audit records; annual review of AI-CAM implementation against program learning goals
Continuous improvement is demonstrated through cycles of assessment and revision	Records of AI policy revisions in response to assessment data; faculty development participation rates; documentation of rubric and syllabus updates across AI-CAM levels

The table above illustrates a principle that institutions found intimidating before it was made explicit: accreditors are not asking new questions about AI. They are asking the same questions they have always asked: outcomes, integrity, faculty authority, effectiveness, and improvement, and expecting that AI integration will appear in the evidence base with the same coherence and intentionality as every other instructional practice. Institutions that treat AI integration as a parallel track, documented separately from their regular assessment and accreditation cycles, create unnecessary complexity and increase the risk of appearing inconsistent under review.

The practical implication is integration, not addition. AI-CAM level documentation should appear in the same course syllabi that accreditors review during comprehensive evaluations. AI literacy outcomes should appear in the same program learning outcome maps that institutional effectiveness officers maintain. AI bias audit records should be filed in the same institutional research repositories as other student outcome data. When AI governance is woven into existing institutional documentation systems rather than maintained separately, it is both more sustainable and more credible under external review.

The Specific Challenge of Programmatic Accreditation

Regional accreditation establishes baseline quality standards for the institution as a whole. Programmatic accreditation – through bodies like AACSB for business, CCNE and ACEN for nursing, CSWE for social work, ABA for law, and CACREP for counseling – establishes field-specific standards that often go further than regional accreditation in specifying curriculum content, assessment methods, and professional competency requirements. AI integration in professionally accredited programs must navigate both levels simultaneously.

Several programmatic accreditors have begun issuing AI-specific guidance, and the pace of that guidance is accelerating. While the specific language of that guidance will continue to evolve, two structural patterns have emerged consistently across programmatic accreditation contexts. First, accreditors are increasingly treating AI literacy as a dimension of professional competency rather than a general academic skill, which means that AI integration at Levels 3 through 6 in professionally accredited programs should be explicitly connected to the program's professional competency framework, not merely to general institutional AI literacy goals. Second, accreditors with strong practice-readiness standards, e.g. nursing, social work, counseling, law, are scrutinizing AI integration for evidence that it strengthens rather than compromises independent professional judgment, which means that the foundational competency protection argument for Level 0 in appropriate professional courses is becoming more, not less, relevant in accredited professional programs.

Sposato (2025) identifies accreditation alignment as one of the primary governance challenges in educational AI leadership, noting that institutions that develop AI integration strategies without mapping them to their specific accreditation obligations risk creating compliance vulnerabilities that become visible, and costly, only at the point of review. The preventive investment is modest: a structured mapping exercise, conducted once per program and updated annually, that connects the program's AI-CAM implementation to its accreditation standards. That mapping, filed with accreditation documentation and reviewed by the program's accreditation liaison, is the single most efficient governance action available to programs operating under programmatic accreditation.

Interdepartmental Coordination and Governance Infrastructure

AI governance in higher education cannot be housed in a single administrative unit. It requires sustained coordination among offices and constituencies whose institutional roles, priorities, and vocabularies rarely overlap in ordinary operations: academic affairs, information technology, legal counsel, institutional research, disability services, student affairs, and faculty governance bodies. The absence of coordination infrastructure produces the fragmented, inconsistent, reactive governance landscape that characterizes most institutions' current AI posture. Its presence enables the coherent, developmental, accreditation-accountable integration that this book advocates.

The AI Integration Governance Committee

The most effective structural solution adopted by institutions that have moved furthest toward coherent AI governance is a standing interdisciplinary AI Integration Governance Committee with a defined membership, clear charge, and regular reporting relationship to both academic affairs leadership and faculty governance. The committee's charge should address four functions: policy development and harmonization, tool review and approval, equity monitoring and bias auditing, and annual review of AI-CAM implementation data.

Membership should include representation from faculty governance, academic affairs, instructional design, IT, legal counsel, student affairs, disability services, and institutional research. Each representative brings a domain expertise that the others lack: legal counsel brings FERPA and Title VI compliance knowledge; disability services brings WCAG accessibility standards expertise; institutional research brings the data infrastructure for outcome monitoring; IT brings the technical capacity to evaluate tool security and data handling; and faculty governance brings the legitimacy that policy adoption requires. No single office can substitute for this combination. Institutions that attempt AI governance through any single office, whether academic affairs, IT, or legal, consistently report the same outcome: policies that are technically sound but practically unsupported, or practically useful but legally exposed.

The Role of Instructional Design in Governance

Instructional designers occupy a uniquely important position in AI governance infrastructure because they sit at the intersection of pedagogical intention and implementation reality. When faculty make AI-CAM-level decisions, instructional designers translate those decisions into course architecture, ensuring that assessment designs match integration levels, that accessibility requirements are met, and that AI tool selections align with both pedagogical goals and institutional approval standards. When accreditation reviewers ask for evidence that AI integration is pedagogically intentional rather than technologically opportunistic, the documentation trail that instructional designers maintain, course redesign records, outcome alignment maps, rubric revision histories, provides that evidence.

Effective technology integration requires more than individual faculty initiative. Bates's approach, as summarized by Kocdar (2017), emphasizes professional development, learning-technology support systems, collaborative teaching structures, and an institution-wide strategy as necessary supports for high-quality teaching in a digital age. Applied to AI governance, this suggests that instructional designers can help faculty translate institutional expectations into pedagogically coherent course and assessment designs. The mechanism is straightforward: when faculty have a knowledgeable partner who helps them navigate AI-CAM level decisions, disclosure standard design, and accreditation documentation simultaneously, the cognitive and administrative burden of responsible integration drops to a level that enables sustained adoption.

Legal and Compliance Coordination

The legal landscape surrounding AI in education is evolving rapidly, and institutions that lack structured legal review of their AI governance decisions will encounter preventable compliance exposures. Several legal domains require ongoing attention. FERPA compliance for student data shared with AI platforms requires legal review of the platform's terms of service before institutional approval. Copyright and intellectual property questions surrounding AI-generated content in academic work remain unsettled in federal case law, and institutional IP policies should be reviewed by legal counsel annually until the legal landscape stabilizes. Title VI and ADA compliance obligations related to algorithmic bias and accessibility require legal counsel familiar with both civil rights law and educational technology to be meaningfully protective.

The legal review function should be proactive rather than reactive.

From Policy to Culture: The Governance Goal

Governance frameworks do not, by themselves, produce the institutional culture in which responsible AI integration becomes self-sustaining. Policy documents establish expectations. Committees establish accountability structures. Accreditation documentation establishes evidence trails. But none of these governance mechanisms produces the shared understanding, professional commitment, and disciplinary seriousness that characterize institutions where AI integration is genuinely working.

The transition from policy compliance to institutional culture requires two things that governance structures alone cannot supply: leadership that articulates why AI literacy matters in relation to the institution's specific mission, and faculty who experience AI governance not as administrative burden but as professional support. Both require intentional investment.

Mission alignment is the most underutilized lever in institutional AI governance. Institutions with clear, specific, publicly articulated accounts of why AI literacy matters for their graduates consistently report higher faculty engagement with AI integration and stronger student understanding of the expectations AI literacy sets for them. A faith-based institution whose AI policy is grounded in its commitment to intellectual integrity and vocational formation is asking something different of its faculty and students than a technical institute whose AI policy is grounded in professional preparation for an AI-shaped workforce. Both accounts are legitimate. Both are more motivating than a policy document that lists permitted and prohibited tools without explaining the educational purpose of the distinction.

Faculty experience of governance as support rather than constraint depends largely on whether governance structures are designed around faculty needs or administrative convenience. Policies that create ambiguity about what constitutes permitted AI use, about how AI-assisted work should be assessed, about what documentation accreditors actually require create anxiety and generate workarounds rather than compliance. Policies that create clarity, provide resources, and reduce the administrative burden of responsible integration create the conditions for genuine faculty engagement. The AI-CAM framework, deployed as an institutional governance vocabulary, is designed to do precisely this: reduce ambiguity without reducing autonomy and create coherence without requiring uniformity.

When governance, culture, and faculty development work together AI integration moves from the reactive, fragmented, anxiety-driven posture that characterizes most institutions' current state to the intentional, developmental, accountable posture that this book argues higher education requires. The AI-CAM framework provides the vocabulary. Governance provides the structure. Culture provides the commitment. Together, they constitute the architecture within which artificial intelligence can serve the educational mission rather than complicate it.

Chapter 15. Demonstrating Institutional Quality

Assessment and Accountability

Assessment is the institutional act by which universities declare what counts as evidence of learning. When the conditions of learning change assessment must change with them or become unreliable. Rubrics designed for single-authorship cannot accurately measure learning in hybrid human-AI production environments. Exams that assess content recall cannot capture the evaluative reasoning that AI-integrated courses are designed to develop. Portfolio criteria that treat writing as a product cannot assess the iterative, reflective process that structured AI collaboration makes visible and important.

The challenge facing higher education is not simply that old assessments fail to account for AI. The deeper challenge is that AI integration, done well, expands what can legitimately be considered evidence of learning, and that expansion requires institutions to articulate, with greater precision than before, what they are actually trying to measure and why. Wiggins (1990) argues that assessment should directly examine students' performance on worthy intellectual tasks rather than rely primarily on simplified proxies for learning. Extending this principle into the digital environment, Andrews et al. (2021) observe that assessment must do more than reproduce traditional practices through new technologies. They note that incorporating AI into assessment can create more authentic tasks when its use reflects the practices and complex judgments students will encounter beyond the university.

This chapter develops a comprehensive framework for assessment design in AI-integrated courses, organized around five dimensions: the theoretical foundation of constructive alignment in AI contexts, the measurement of disciplinary mastery alongside AI literacy, the design of rubrics for hybrid authorship, process documentation as evidence of learning, and the institutional requirements of validity, reliability, and accreditation accountability. Throughout, the AI-Course Application Matrix (AI-CAM) provides the structural reference point: assessment practices should be calibrated to the designated level of AI integration, and that calibration should be explicit, documented, and defensible.

Rethinking Constructive Alignment in AI-Integrated Environments

Constructive alignment, the principle that learning outcomes, learning activities, and assessment tasks should reinforce one another in a coherent system, was articulated by Biggs (1996) and has become a foundational principle of higher education curriculum design. Its application to AI-integrated courses is not merely an extension of existing practice. It requires a genuine rethinking of what alignment means when AI tools participate in the learning activities that assessment is designed to evaluate.

In a traditional constructively aligned course, the learning activity (writing a research paper) and the assessment task (evaluating that paper) share the same object: the student's independent intellectual work. In an AI-integrated course at Levels 3 through 6, the learning activity includes AI engagement, and the assessment task must therefore evaluate not only the product of that engagement but the quality of the engagement itself. Alignment in this context requires that assessments explicitly address the AI-mediated dimensions of the learning activity as an integrated component of it.

Boud and Dawson (2023) argue that assessment in AI-augmented environments must shift from verifying knowledge possession to evaluating knowledge application in complex, authentic conditions, conditions that increasingly include AI tools as part of the professional landscape students are being prepared to enter. This shift has direct implications for AI-CAM level selection: the assessment design appropriate for a Level 4 course, where AI literacy is an explicit learning outcome, cannot be the same as that for a Level 0 course, where independent cognitive performance is the organizing purpose.

The practical implication is that faculty must make AI-CAM level designation an active input into assessment design, not a policy label attached to the syllabus after the course is designed. The question 'At what level of AI integration is this course operating?' must be followed immediately by the question 'And what does that level require of my assessment instruments?'

Measuring Disciplinary Mastery and AI Literacy as Distinct Competencies

One of the most consequential design decisions in AI-integrated assessment is whether disciplinary mastery and AI literacy are measured together or separately. The answer depends on the AI-CAM level and the specific learning outcomes of the course, but the principle is consistent: conflating the two produces assessment that is unreliable for both.

Disciplinary mastery is what higher education has always assessed. AI literacy, the ability to prompt effectively, evaluate outputs critically, detect bias, verify claims, document usage, and exercise professional judgment in AI-mediated contexts, is a newer and distinct competency. A student who is highly fluent with AI tools but weak in disciplinary reasoning should not receive the same assessment result as a student who is deeply competent in the discipline but appropriately cautious with AI tools. Conversely, a student with strong disciplinary knowledge who cannot evaluate AI outputs critically is not fully prepared for the professional environments that increasingly require that evaluative capacity.

Chen et al. (2025) found that students who demonstrated high AI tool adoption did not necessarily demonstrate higher-order critical evaluation of AI outputs. This suggests that frequency of use and quality of engagement are distinct dimensions that require separate measurement. This finding has direct implications for rubric design: an assessment that measures only whether AI was used, or only how the disciplinary product turned out, misses the most important dimension of what AI-integrated learning is designed to develop.

At AI-CAM Levels 0 through 2, disciplinary mastery is the primary assessment domain, with AI literacy either absent (Level 0) or assessed through transparency criteria (Levels 1–2). At Levels 3 through 6, both domains require explicit rubric criteria. The weighting of those criteria should reflect the course's designated outcomes, a Level 4 course with AI literacy embedded as a primary outcome may weight AI literacy criteria at 30 to 40 percent of the total assessment, while a Level 3 course using a single required AI assignment may weight AI literacy criteria at 20 to 25 percent for that specific assignment.

Rubric Design for Hybrid Authorship

The traditional rubric assumes a single author. Its criteria assess the author's argument, evidence, organization, style, and command of disciplinary conventions. When authorship becomes hybrid, when human reasoning and AI assistance interact in the production of assessed work, traditional rubrics become inadequate in specific and predictable ways. They cannot distinguish between a well-organized argument the student constructed and one generated by the AI. They cannot identify whether analytical claims reflect genuine disciplinary reasoning or plausible-sounding AI output. They cannot assess whether the student exercised evaluative judgment over AI contributions or accepted them uncritically.

Designing rubrics for hybrid authorship requires criteria that are largely invisible in traditional assessment contexts but central to AI-integrated learning. Wiggins (1990) argues that authentic assessment depends upon appropriate criteria for evaluating varied products and should require students to produce polished, thorough, and justifiable work. Andrews et al. (2021) similarly emphasize student agency, critical engagement with technology, ethical considerations, and alignment between assessment and digital practices beyond the university. Building on these principles, AI-CAM rubrics should address three additional dimensions: the degree of human intellectual contribution to the final product, the quality of human oversight and evaluation of AI-generated content, and the transparency and professional integrity of the AI-engagement process. These dimensions supplement rather than replace disciplinary assessment criteria.

The following rubric illustrates these principles for a Level 4 analytical writing assignment in a social science course. Note that intellectual contribution and AI evaluation criteria are weighted alongside disciplinary criteria, not added as afterthoughts.

Sample Rubric: AI-Integrated Analytical Essay (Level 4)

Criterion	Unsatisfactory (1)	Developing (2)	Proficient (3)	Exemplary (4)
Disciplinary Analysis	Claims are unsupported or factually inaccurate. Disciplinary concepts are absent or misapplied.	Claims are present but underdeveloped. Disciplinary concepts are referenced but not applied with precision.	Claims are supported with appropriate evidence. Disciplinary concepts are applied accurately and with reasonable depth.	Claims are sophisticated, well-evidenced, and demonstrate original analytical synthesis within disciplinary standards.
Intellectual Contribution	No evidence of original analysis beyond AI-generated content. The submission reads as unrevised AI output.	Some original framing is present but the student's analytical contribution is difficult to distinguish from AI-	The student's intellectual contribution is clearly identifiable. AI-generated content has been substantially revised,	The student's voice, judgment, and disciplinary reasoning are consistently evident. AI contributions are clearly

		generated content.	reframed, or extended.	subordinate to and shaped by the student's intellectual purpose.
Critical Evaluation of AI Output	AI outputs are accepted without evaluation. Errors, biases, or limitations are not identified or addressed.	Some evaluation of AI outputs is present but superficial. Significant limitations are unaddressed.	AI outputs are evaluated with reasonable critical attention. At least one limitation, error, or bias is identified and addressed in the submission.	AI outputs are rigorously evaluated. Multiple limitations are identified, addressed, and integrated into a reflective account of AI's contribution to the work.
Transparency and Documentation	AI use is not disclosed or documentation is absent. It is impossible to determine how AI was used.	AI use is disclosed but documentation is incomplete or inconsistent with the submission's content.	AI use is fully disclosed with a clear account of tools used, purposes served, and degree of integration.	Documentation is thorough and professionally formatted. The AI usage account is detailed enough to be reproduced and provides a

				complete audit trail of the analytical process.
Ethical Compliance	Submission violates course AI policy. Authorship boundaries are unclear or misrepresented.	Submission is largely compliant but reflects uncertainty about authorship boundaries or disclosure standards.	Submission is fully compliant with course AI policy. Authorship boundaries are respected and clearly communicated.	Submission demonstrates sophisticated ethical awareness. The student articulates the basis for their AI engagement decisions and reflects on the professional implications.

This rubric structure can be adapted across disciplines and AI-CAM levels by adjusting the weight of each criterion and the specific descriptors within each dimension. At Level 2, the Intellectual Contribution and Critical Evaluation criteria may carry lower weight. At Level 5 or 6, they should carry the highest weight for any criterion in the rubric, because evaluative judgment in AI collaboration is the competency the course is most centrally designed to develop.

Process Documentation as Evidence of Learning

One of the shifts AI integration enables in assessment is the shift from product-only to process-inclusive evaluation. AI integration makes learning processes more visible and that visibility can be turned into evidence of learning in ways that product-only assessment cannot capture.

Yan et al. (2024) argue that process-oriented assessment in AI-integrated courses provides evidence of the metacognitive competencies, self-monitoring, evaluative reasoning, and adaptive revision that are most predictive of long-term academic and professional success and most difficult to assess through traditional product-based methods. When a student's prompt log shows progressive refinement of their AI queries over successive iterations, that log is evidence of developing analytical sophistication that the final product alone cannot reveal.

Process documentation formats vary by course level and disciplinary context, but several have demonstrated broad applicability across AI-CAM levels. Prompt iteration logs are appropriate from Level 3 onward and require minimal additional student effort when built into assignment instructions from the outset. Comparative draft analysis is appropriate at Levels 2 through 5 and provides direct evidence of intellectual contribution. Validation reports are particularly important at Levels 3 through 6 and directly connect to the professional accountability standards of most disciplines.

Faculty new to process-inclusive assessment sometimes express concern that documenting the process adds to students' workload without a commensurate educational benefit. The evidence does not support this concern when process documentation is designed as a learning activity rather than an administrative requirement. When students know they will be asked to explain their revision decisions, they make them more deliberate. When they know they will be asked to document their fact-checking procedures, they fact-check more rigorously. The documentation requirement changes the behavior it is designed to reveal, which is precisely what good assessment design should do.

Validity, Reliability, and Authentic Assessment in AI Contexts

The introduction of AI into assessed work creates new threats to both validity and reliability that assessment designers must address explicitly. Validity requires that an assessment measures what it claims to measure. Reliability requires consistency across students, sections, and evaluators. Both are complicated by AI integration in specific ways that traditional assessment quality frameworks did not anticipate.

The primary validity threat in AI-integrated assessment is construct contamination: the risk that assessment results reflect AI tool proficiency rather than the disciplinary or AI literacy competencies the assessment is designed to measure. A student with advanced prompting skills may produce a higher-quality analytical essay at a lower level of actual disciplinary understanding than a student with weaker prompting skills but stronger disciplinary knowledge. If the rubric cannot distinguish between these students. i.e. if it rewards the product without assessing the process that produced it, then it has a validity problem. The solution is not to prohibit AI use but to design assessments that require higher-order reasoning that AI tools cannot supply: synthesis across sources, application of disciplinary judgment to specific contextual conditions, or defense of analytical choices under questioning.

The primary reliability threat in AI-integrated assessment is evaluator inconsistency in interpreting hybrid authorship criteria. When rubrics include criteria such as 'evidence of original intellectual contribution,' evaluators may apply very different standards, particularly in disciplines without established norms for assessing AI-assisted work. Institutions addressing this challenge have found that calibration sessions in which faculty evaluate sample submissions together, discuss disagreements, and develop shared interpretive standards significantly improve inter-rater reliability for hybrid authorship criteria (Boud & Dawson, 2023). Calibration should be built into faculty development programs for AI-integrated courses rather than treated as an optional professional development activity.

Authentic assessment has long been advocated as a more valid alternative to decontextualized testing (Wiggins, 1990). AI integration strengthens the case for authentic assessment by making decontextualized testing easier to game: a student who can use AI to complete an isolated analytical task in an academic format may not be able to apply that analysis in a professional context requiring judgment, accountability, and communication with non-academic audiences. Designing authentic assessment tasks that require AI-integrated professional reasoning provides both higher validity and stronger preparation for the professional environments graduates will enter.

Documentation, Accreditation, and Institutional Accountability

Accrediting bodies across higher education have begun issuing guidance on AI integration that has direct implications for assessment documentation. The Higher Learning Commission, SACSCOC, AACSB, CCNE, and other regional and programmatic accreditors share a common expectation: that institutions can demonstrate coherent, intentional, and evidence-based approaches to student learning assessment. AI integration, precisely because it alters the conditions under which learning occurs and is evaluated, heightens the documentation burden without changing the fundamental accountability standard.

Sposato (2025) identifies assessment transparency as one of the primary governance challenges introduced by AI integration in higher education. Assessment systems designed before AI tools were widely available may produce outcome data that is no longer interpretable in the same way, because the conditions of production have changed without corresponding changes to the assessment instruments or documentation practices.

Institutions building AI-responsive assessment systems should ensure that their documentation includes: AI-CAM level designations in course syllabi, with rationale for level selection; alignment maps showing how AI literacy outcomes connect to program and institutional learning goals; samples of AI disclosure statements and their connection to assessed criteria; rubric revision records demonstrating how assessment instruments have been updated to reflect AI integration levels; and evidence of faculty calibration and inter-rater reliability processes for hybrid authorship criteria. This documentation should be maintained at both the course and program levels and integrated into the institution's regular assessment reporting cycles, rather than treated as a separate AI compliance activity.

Assessment is how institutions make their educational commitments visible and accountable. In AI-integrated courses, it is also how institutions demonstrate that AI serves learning rather than replacing it. A well-designed, well-documented assessment system for an AI-integrated curriculum is not merely good academic practice. It is institutional evidence that the integration has been designed with intellectual seriousness, and that seriousness is precisely what accreditors, employers, and the students themselves have a right to expect.

Chapter 16. Building Institutional Resilience

Equity, Access, and Human Flourishing

The promise of AI integration in higher education including, personalized learning, scalable feedback, and expanded access to high-quality instructional support is real. So is the risk that AI integration, implemented without deliberate attention to equity, will reproduce and amplify the inequities already present in higher education rather than mitigate them. Those two realities coexist, and institutions that attend only to the promise without reckoning with the risk will find themselves having accelerated the very disparities they aspire to reduce.

Equity in AI-integrated higher education is not a single problem with a single solution. It is a cluster of related but distinct challenges that manifest differently across student populations, institutional contexts, and the specific AI tools and integration approaches in use. This chapter addresses four dimensions of that cluster: the digital divide and differential access to AI tools and the literacies required to use them effectively; accessibility obligations under disability law and the specific challenges AI tools create for students with disabilities; algorithmic bias and the ways AI systems can disadvantage students based on race, language background, and cultural context; and the structural design commitments that equity-centered AI integration requires at the institutional level.

Across these dimensions, the governing principle is the same: equity in AI integration is a design responsibility, not an afterthought. Institutions that build equity considerations into the initial architecture of AI-integrated courses will produce better outcomes than those that identify equity problems after implementation and attempt to retrofit solutions.

Equity and AI-Integrated Dimensions

The Digital Divide: Beyond Device Access

The digital divide in AI-integrated higher education is frequently framed as a hardware and connectivity problem: students who lack reliable devices or broadband access cannot use AI tools and therefore cannot benefit from or participate in AI-integrated coursework. This framing is accurate as far as it goes, but it understates the scope of the problem.

Device and connectivity access are necessary conditions for using AI tools, but not sufficient for equitable AI-integrated learning. Research consistently identifies a second-level digital divide, what Hargittai (2002) termed the difference between access and use, that operates independently of hardware availability. Students who have physical access to AI tools may lack the prompting literacy, evaluative frameworks, and metacognitive habits required to use those tools in ways that produce genuine learning rather than superficial output.

A third level of the digital divide operates at the level of social capital: the informal networks through which students learn about AI tools, discover effective prompting strategies, and develop the habit of integrating AI assistance into academic workflows. Students with high social capital, those connected to peer networks, family members, or professional contacts who use AI tools fluently, develop AI literacy through informal channels that are invisible to institutions and unavailable to students whose social networks do not include AI-fluent members. This informal channel amplifies rather than compensates for formal educational gaps.

The implication for AI-integrated course design is that institutions cannot assume that making AI tools available is equivalent to providing equitable access to AI-integrated learning. Scaffolded instruction in AI tool use, such as prompt construction, output evaluation, disciplinary application, ethical disclosure, must be built into courses at Levels 2 through 6, not treated as background knowledge students are expected to bring. Failure to provide this scaffolding does not protect equity-vulnerable students from AI's risks. It ensures that more advantaged students benefit from AI integration while less advantaged students are left navigating the tools without guidance, producing lower-quality outcomes and reinforcing the very disparities that structured integration is designed to address.

Equity Design Principle 1: Scaffold AI Literacy Explicitly

Do not assume that permitting AI tool use is equivalent to providing equitable access to AI-integrated learning. Build explicit instruction in prompt construction, output evaluation, and disciplinary application into every course operating at Level 2 or above. Students who receive this scaffolding outperform those who do not, and the benefit is largest for students with the least prior AI experience.

Accessibility, Disability, and Legal Obligations

AI integration in higher education intersects with disability law in ways that create both obligations and opportunities for institutions. Section 504 of the Rehabilitation Act of 1973 and Title II of the Americans with Disabilities Act require that educational programs be accessible to students with disabilities. The integration of AI tools into coursework does not suspend these obligations, it extends them into new domains.

Digital flexibility should not be confused with automatic accessibility. Moore (2007) cautions that digital environments can remain as inaccessible as physical environments when accessibility is not deliberately incorporated into their design. Accessibility review must therefore encompass the AI tool, the learning activity, the assessment process, and the larger institutional systems within which they operate.

The accessibility obligations created by AI integration fall into three categories. First, the AI tools themselves must be accessible. Tools that rely on visual interfaces without screen reader compatibility, audio outputs without captioning, or interaction models that require fine motor control without alternatives exclude students with sensory or physical disabilities from full participation in AI-integrated learning activities. Institutions that mandate or strongly encourage the use of AI tools in coursework bear responsibility for ensuring that those tools meet the Web Content Accessibility Guidelines (WCAG 2.1 AA). This responsibility cannot be delegated entirely to third-party vendors without institutional review and monitoring (U.S. Department of Education, 2023).

Second, the assessments designed for AI-integrated courses must be accessible. When process documentation becomes part of the assessed work, institutions must ensure that documentation requirements do not create disproportionate barriers for students with learning disabilities, cognitive processing differences, or language-based disabilities. Extended time accommodations, alternative documentation formats, and assistive technology compatibility should be addressed in the assessment design phase rather than retrofitted after the fact.

Third, and perhaps most importantly, AI tools themselves can function as accessibility supports for students with disabilities when they are designed and deployed with that purpose in mind. Text-to-speech, speech-to-text, real-time grammar and syntax feedback, and AI-assisted organizational scaffolding can meaningfully reduce barriers for students with dyslexia, ADHD, processing disorders, and other learning differences. Rose and Meyer's (2002) Universal Design for Learning framework, which advocates for multiple means of representation, expression, and engagement, finds a new application in AI-integrated course design: AI tools can provide multiple pathways to the same learning goal, increasing accessibility for students whose learning profiles are poorly served by traditional single-mode instruction.

The practical implication is that accessibility review should be a standard component of AI-integrated course design at every level. Faculty working with institutional accessibility offices to review AI tool selection, assessment design, and documentation requirements before implementation, rather than after students with disabilities have already encountered barriers, is a legal obligation with institutional liability implications.

Equity Design Principle 2: Accessibility Is Pre-Implementation Work

Conduct accessibility review of AI tools and assessment designs before the course launches, not after students with disabilities report barriers. Review should address: (1) WCAG 2.1 AA compliance of AI tools, (2) accommodation compatibility of process documentation requirements, and (3) opportunity to deploy AI as an accessibility support — not only as a content tool — for students with learning differences.

Algorithmic Bias and the Unequal Distribution of AI Error

AI tools trained on large text corpora inherit the biases present in those corpora. This is not a temporary limitation of current technology that future models will resolve. It is a structural feature of how language models work: they learn statistical patterns from human-generated text, and human-generated text reflects the inequities, stereotypes, power dynamics, and representational gaps of the societies in which it was produced. The specific manifestations of algorithmic bias most relevant to higher education include language bias, cultural bias, and representational bias, and their consequences are not uniformly distributed across student populations.

Language bias in AI tools is among the most extensively documented equity concerns in educational technology. Large language models perform significantly better on text written in Standard American English than on text written in African American Vernacular English, non-native English patterns, or regional and dialectal variations (Blodgett et al., 2020). When AI writing feedback tools evaluate student prose, they systematically rate non-dominant English varieties as lower quality because the models were trained on corpora that overrepresent dominant language norms. Students whose primary linguistic identity is not Standard American English receive feedback that penalizes their language identity and may pressure them toward linguistic assimilation rather than developing a code-switching competency grounded in genuine bilingual or bidialectal ability.

Cultural bias in AI tools manifests in the content and framing of AI-generated analyses, arguments, and examples. When students from non-Western, non-Christian, or non-dominant cultural backgrounds use AI tools to generate or evaluate content relevant to their cultural contexts, those tools frequently produce outputs that center Western, Eurocentric, or secular assumptions because its training data reflects the representational inequities of globally dominant media and academic publishing. A theology student from a Pentecostal tradition, a nursing student from a collectivist cultural background, or a business student from a non-Western market context may find that AI tools systematically produce content that misrepresents or ignores their disciplinary and cultural frame of reference.

Representational bias, the underrepresentation of certain communities, perspectives, and knowledge traditions in AI training data, affects the quality and reliability of AI outputs for students from those communities in ways that their more advantaged peers do not experience. This is a distributional equity problem: AI integration does not introduce a uniform risk to all students. It introduces larger risks to students who are already marginalized within the representational norms of dominant academic culture.

Faculty designing AI-integrated courses have several practical responses available. Making algorithmic bias an explicit topic of instruction gives all students the analytical tools to identify and correct for bias in AI outputs. Requiring students to evaluate AI outputs against their own cultural and disciplinary knowledge rather than accepting AI authority positions students as experts on their own contexts. Selecting AI tools with demonstrated attention to bias mitigation and transparent documentation of training data provides at least partial protection against the most egregious representational failures. And building cultural and linguistic diversity explicitly into the course's AI engagement framework such as asking students to test AI tools on content drawn from their own cultural contexts and to report on the quality of the outputs turns a structural limitation into a pedagogical resource.

Equity Design Principle 3: Teach Algorithmic Bias as Disciplinary Content

Do not treat AI bias as a background disclaimer. Make it explicit disciplinary content at Levels 3 and above. Require students to test AI tools on content from their own cultural, linguistic, and disciplinary contexts and to evaluate the quality of outputs against their own knowledge. This practice develops critical AI literacy while validating students' own expertise as an evaluative resource.

Prompt Literacy as a New Dimension of Educational Inequality

Among the least discussed yet most consequential equity dimensions of AI integration is what researchers have begun to call the prompt literacy gap: the systematic difference in the quality of AI outputs that students receive, depending on how effectively they can formulate prompts (Lo, 2023). AI tools do not respond uniformly to all prompts. Well-constructed prompts produce meaningfully higher-quality outputs than vague or poorly constructed prompts. The skill of effective prompt construction is, in this sense, a form of intellectual capital that produces differential returns from the same AI tool.

Like other forms of intellectual capital, prompt literacy is not equally distributed. It correlates with educational background, English language proficiency, prior exposure to AI tools, and access to informal coaching from more experienced users. Students who arrive at college with strong prompt literacy will extract more value from AI integration than students who arrive without it. If institutions treat prompt literacy as a background assumption rather than a taught competency, AI integration will serve to reproduce and amplify existing educational inequities rather than mitigate them.

The solution is straightforward in principle and requires genuine commitment in practice: prompt literacy instruction must be built into AI-integrated courses as an explicit learning activity, not mentioned once in a syllabus and assumed thereafter. Chen et al. (2025) approach generative AI literacy as a multidimensional capacity involving how students adopt and interact with AI, evaluate its outputs, and understand the ethical implications of its use. This broader conception suggests that functional familiarity with an AI tool is not sufficient evidence of AI literacy.

Within AI-CAM, students therefore need scaffolded practice in prompt construction, instructor feedback on prompt quality, opportunities for iterative refinement, and explicit instruction in critically evaluating the resulting outputs.

Structural Commitments for Equity-Centered AI Integration

The four equity dimensions addressed above, the multilevel digital divide, disability accessibility obligations, algorithmic bias, and the prompt literacy gap, share a common structural feature: they cannot be adequately addressed by individual faculty members' good intentions or course-level accommodations alone. They require institutional commitments that create the conditions for equitable AI integration before individual courses are designed and after they are delivered.

Those structural commitments fall into four categories. Technology provisioning must ensure that all students have reliable access to the AI tools required for coursework, regardless of whether they own a personal device or have home internet connectivity. Institutions that require AI tools in courses but do not provide device lending programs, campus AI access points, or institutional tool subscriptions are creating legally and ethically problematic access barriers. Faculty development must include explicit training in equity-centered AI integration as a substantive competency domain of equal weight to pedagogical integration design and assessment alignment. Without this training, equity considerations will remain conceptually acknowledged but practically absent from course design decisions.

Curriculum governance must include equity review as a standard component of AI-integrated course approval processes. When courses are redesigned to incorporate AI at Levels 3 through 6, the redesign should be reviewed for accessibility compliance, algorithmic bias implications, and prompt-literacy scaffolding before approval, the same way courses are reviewed for academic integrity standards and learning-outcome alignment. And data monitoring must track AI-integrated course outcomes disaggregated by race, income level, first-generation status, disability status, and language background, so that equity gaps created or exacerbated by AI integration are identified and addressed rather than remaining invisible in aggregated outcome data.

A Framework for Equity-Centered AI-CAM Implementation

Equity in AI integration is a dimension of implementation at every level, rather than a constraint on the AI-CAM framework. At Level 0, equity means ensuring that in-class assessment constraints do not create disproportionate barriers for students with disabilities who lack appropriate accommodations. At Levels 1 and 2, it means scaffolding AI disclosure and tool use so that students with less prior experience are not disadvantaged by familiarity gaps. At Levels 3 and 4, it means teaching algorithmic bias as disciplinary content and requiring students to evaluate AI outputs critically rather than deferring to them. At Levels 5 and 6, it means building accessibility review and equity monitoring into the course architecture as ongoing institutional obligations.

Medina-Gual et al. (2025) found distinct AI-literacy profiles associated with gender and academic stage, while also finding consistently weak socio-critical performance across the sample. Although the study's single-institution context limits generalization, its findings demonstrate why institutions should assess student competencies rather than assume that technological familiarity is evenly distributed.

The AI-Course Application Matrix, aligned with the C.L.E.A.R. framework and implemented with deliberate attention to equity at every level, provides the structural architecture for that simultaneous achievement. Equity-centered AI integration does not require choosing between educational quality and educational justice. When well designed, it demands both and produces graduates equipped to navigate, evaluate, and ethically govern AI tools in the diverse and unequal professional environments they will enter.

Part IV. Future Directions

Chapter 17: The Architectural University

A New Educational Paradigm

The Moment Before Higher Education

Every generation of higher education eventually reaches a moment when it must reconsider not only the tools available for teaching but also the assumptions that have quietly guided educational practice for many years. These moments rarely announce themselves with complete clarity. They emerge gradually as familiar approaches prove less adequate to new realities, prompting institutions to decide whether to respond with isolated adjustments or with a more comprehensive reconsideration of their educational mission.

Artificial intelligence represents such a moment.

Throughout this book, I have argued that the emergence of generative AI should not be understood primarily as a technological event. Universities have always adapted to technological change. The printing press altered access to knowledge. Industrialization reshaped professional education. Digital networks transformed research, communication, and scholarly collaboration. Each innovation required meaningful institutional adaptation, yet none altered the fundamental purpose of higher education. Universities remained responsible for cultivating disciplined inquiry, ethical judgment, intellectual maturity, and preparing graduates capable of contributing thoughtfully to society.

Artificial intelligence does not alter that responsibility. It does, however, require institutions to reconsider how those responsibilities are carried out within a learning environment increasingly shaped by intelligent technologies.

That distinction has guided every chapter of this volume. The central question has never been whether artificial intelligence should be embraced or resisted. Nor has the objective been to identify the most technologically sophisticated approach to course design. Instead, the larger question has remained remarkably consistent: How should higher education respond to artificial intelligence in ways that remain faithful to its enduring educational purposes?

The pace of innovation naturally encourages institutions to focus on immediate questions. Which platforms should be adopted? Which uses should be permitted? How should academic integrity policies be revised? What professional development should faculty receive? These are important questions, and institutions cannot avoid them. Yet they remain secondary questions. They concern implementation rather than purpose.

When institutions begin with implementation, they often discover that each technological advance requires another round of policy revision, another cycle of faculty training, and another set of institutional adjustments. Artificial intelligence has become something that must be continually managed because no broader educational framework exists through which new developments can be interpreted. The institution remains responsive, but its responses are largely reactive.

An architectural approach begins elsewhere. It first asks which forms of intellectual development remain essential regardless of technological change. It asks which aspects of learning require independent cognitive performance, where thoughtful technological support may strengthen learning, how professional judgment should develop across a curriculum, and what responsibilities graduates will carry into increasingly AI-mediated professions. Once those questions have been answered, decisions regarding particular technologies become considerably clearer because they are evaluated against educational purposes that remain stable even as technological capabilities continue to evolve.

The AI-Course Application Matrix was developed as one expression of that architectural way of thinking. Although the framework emerged in response to artificial intelligence, its underlying logic extends beyond any single technology. At its heart, AI-CAM is a developmental framework. It assumes that students require different instructional environments at different stages of learning and that educational decisions should always be governed by developmental readiness rather than technological possibility. Artificial intelligence provided the immediate context for articulating that progression, but the progression itself reflects longstanding principles of sound curriculum design.

For that reason, I hope readers will ultimately regard AI-CAM as more than a framework for AI integration. Its greater contribution, if it proves useful, may be that it encourages institutions to recover a developmental understanding of curriculum at precisely the moment when technological change makes such thinking increasingly necessary. The seven levels are less important than the educational philosophy they represent. They remind us that learning proceeds through stages, that instructional design should reflect those stages, and that technologies should serve rather than determine the developmental work of education.

Seen from this perspective, the present moment becomes less a crisis to be managed than an opportunity to think more carefully about the nature of higher education itself.

Artificial intelligence has exposed questions that were often present long before generative AI appeared in our classrooms. How do we distinguish performance from genuine understanding? What evidence demonstrates authentic learning? Which forms of knowledge require direct personal engagement before technological assistance becomes appropriate? What kinds of judgment remain uniquely human, even as increasingly capable technologies participate in professional work? These questions have always existed beneath the surface of curriculum design. Artificial intelligence has simply brought them into sharper focus.

There is, therefore, a certain irony in the current conversation. Much of the public discussion surrounding AI assumes that universities are facing an unprecedented technological challenge. In one sense, that is certainly true. Yet the deeper challenge confronting higher education is not technological at all. It is educational. Institutions are once again being asked to articulate what they believe the university exists to accomplish and to ensure that their instructional practices remain aligned with that purpose.

History suggests that universities have been at their strongest when they have responded to periods of significant change by returning to first principles rather than abandoning them. They have adapted methods while preserving the mission. They have incorporated new tools without allowing those tools to redefine education itself. They have remained remarkably durable because their deepest commitments have never depended upon the technologies available in a particular historical moment.

The same opportunity exists today.

Artificial intelligence undoubtedly changes the conditions under which teaching and learning take place. It changes professional practice across many disciplines. It changes some of the competencies graduates will need. It even changes some of the assumptions upon which traditional assessment has been built. None of those changes, however, diminishes the university's central responsibility. If anything, they make that responsibility more obvious. As information becomes easier to generate, disciplined judgment becomes more valuable. As automated systems become more persuasive, careful evaluation becomes essential, not optional. As technological capability expands, the need for intellectual maturity, ethical reasoning, and professional wisdom becomes increasingly important, not less.

The question before higher education, therefore, is not whether artificial intelligence will continue to evolve. It undoubtedly will. The more enduring question is whether institutions will respond to that evolution through a succession of isolated technological adjustments or through a coherent educational vision capable of guiding decisions long after today's AI systems have been replaced by others not yet imagined.

That is the larger argument toward which this book has been moving from the beginning. Artificial intelligence is not asking higher education to become something fundamentally different, rather it is inviting higher education to become more intentional about what it has always been called to do.

That invitation naturally leads to the next question. If universities choose to think architecturally rather than reactively, what kind of institution begins to emerge? What does an educational philosophy grounded in intentional design actually look like when it shapes the life of an institution?

Those questions shift our attention from the immediate challenges of AI adoption to the broader vision of the architectural university.

Architecture as an Educational Philosophy

The language of architecture has appeared repeatedly throughout this book because it describes something more enduring than the integration of artificial intelligence. It offers a way of thinking about educational design itself.

Architecture is concerned with relationships. An architect does not begin by selecting materials. The process begins with purpose. Only after the purpose of a building has been carefully considered do questions of structure, function, circulation, aesthetics, and materials become meaningful. Every subsequent decision derives its significance from the larger vision the structure is intended to serve.

Curriculum design follows much the same pattern.

Learning outcomes, instructional strategies, assessment practices, educational technologies, faculty development, academic policies, and institutional governance are not independent educational activities. They are components of a larger educational structure whose effectiveness depends upon the coherence of the relationships among them. When those relationships are intentional, students experience a curriculum that develops naturally from one stage of learning to the next. When they are not, even well-designed courses can feel disconnected from one another because each reflects a different understanding of the educational enterprise. Artificial intelligence has exposed the importance of this coherence with unusual clarity.

Before generative AI became widely available, institutions often tolerated considerable inconsistency across courses. Differences in teaching style, assessment practice, and instructional philosophy certainly existed, but students generally moved through their programs without encountering fundamentally different assumptions about the role of technology in learning. Artificial intelligence has changed that landscape. Students may now encounter complete prohibition in one course, unrestricted use in another, structured collaboration in a third, and AI-integrated assessment in a fourth. Each approach may be individually defensible. Collectively, however, they invite an important question: what educational philosophy connects these experiences into a coherent curriculum? The answer cannot simply be institutional uniformity.

One of higher education's enduring strengths has always been its respect for disciplinary diversity and faculty expertise. A chemistry laboratory, a first-year writing course, a graduate nursing seminar, and a theology capstone should not look identical, as they serve different educational purposes. Architecture does not eliminate those differences. It gives them coherence by ensuring that each course intentionally contributes to the larger developmental journey students experience throughout the program.

This understanding also explains why the AI-Course Application Matrix was never intended to function as a hierarchy.

The seven levels do not describe increasing educational quality. They describe different developmental environments within which learning may occur. A thoughtfully designed Level 0 course and a thoughtfully designed Level 6 course may represent equally sophisticated educational work because each has aligned instructional design with the developmental needs of its students. The distinction lies not in the amount of artificial intelligence incorporated into the course but in the educational purpose the course serves within the curriculum as a whole.

That principle extends well beyond AI integration.

Educational architecture encourages faculty to ask a different set of questions than those that often dominate conversations about innovation. Rather than asking whether a new technology should be adopted, faculty begin by asking what kind of intellectual formation a particular course exists to cultivate. They then consider which instructional practices—including the use or non-use of artificial intelligence—best support that developmental purpose. Technology becomes one educational resource among many rather than the organizing principle of curriculum design.

The implications for institutional leadership are equally important. Universities frequently experience technological change as a succession of initiatives. One innovation follows another. New platforms are introduced, professional development is organized, policies are revised, and strategic plans are updated. While each initiative may be valuable, the cumulative effect can be a growing sense that institutions are continually responding to external developments rather than pursuing a coherent educational vision of their own.

Architecture offers a different posture. Instead of organizing institutional life around successive technological innovations, educational architecture provides a stable framework for evaluating new developments. Emerging technologies become occasions for renewed educational judgment rather than catalysts for institutional disruption. Faculty can ask whether a particular innovation advances the curriculum's developmental purposes because those purposes have already been clearly articulated. The institution responds thoughtfully rather than reactively because its educational philosophy guides its decisions.

This is one reason I have become increasingly convinced that the long-term significance of AI-CAM extends beyond artificial intelligence itself.

The framework proposes a way of thinking about educational change that remains applicable even after today's AI systems have been replaced by technologies we cannot yet anticipate. The particular examples will inevitably evolve. Professional expectations will continue to shift. New instructional possibilities will emerge. Yet the underlying educational questions remain remarkably consistent. What knowledge should students develop independently? When does collaboration become educationally beneficial? How should assessment demonstrate genuine learning? How can institutions preserve coherent developmental pathways while adapting to changing professional realities?

These questions do not belong exclusively to the present moment. They are enduring questions of curriculum design. Artificial intelligence has simply given higher education an opportunity to reconsider itself with renewed seriousness.

Perhaps that is the most important contribution architecture offers as an educational philosophy. It reminds us that the identity of the university should rest instead in the clarity with which it understands its educational mission and the intentionality with which every aspect of institutional life serves that mission.

When institutions begin thinking in these terms, an interesting shift occurs. Artificial intelligence is gradually becoming less the subject of conversation. Attention turns instead to the kind of university educators are trying to build, the kind of graduates they hope to form, and the educational culture that best supports those aspirations.

Technology assumes its proper place—not as the center of institutional identity, but as one element within a much larger vision of human learning.

It is within that larger vision that the idea of the architectural university begins to emerge. Rather than viewing curriculum, faculty work, assessment, governance, and technology as separate institutional concerns, the architectural university understands them as interdependent expressions of a single educational purpose. The institution becomes coherent not because every part is identical, but because every part is intentionally ordered toward the same enduring mission.

The Architectural University

If architecture becomes the governing philosophy of educational design, it inevitably shapes more than individual courses. Over time, it begins to shape the institution's character.

This influence does not emerge through a single initiative, a revised policy, or the adoption of a new technology. It develops gradually as countless educational decisions begin reflecting a shared understanding of the university's purpose. Faculty design courses with greater intentionality. Departments coordinate learning more thoughtfully across programs. Assessment increasingly measures what the institution genuinely values. Professional development reinforces rather than competes with curricular priorities. Governance becomes less concerned with regulating individual practices and more concerned with sustaining educational coherence.

The result is what might appropriately be described as an architectural university.

Such a university should not be understood as a different type of institution. It may be a community college, a liberal arts college, a research university, a seminary, or a professional school. Nor is architectural thinking tied to a particular institutional mission, theological tradition, or organizational structure. Rather, it describes an institution whose educational decisions consistently emerge from a clearly articulated philosophy of learning rather than from technological change alone.

The defining characteristic of an architectural university is intentionality.

Faculty understand how individual courses contribute to larger patterns of student development. Departments recognize how disciplinary learning fits within broader institutional goals. Students encounter expectations that develop logically across the curriculum rather than shifting unpredictably from one classroom to another. Innovation remains welcome, but it occurs within an educational framework that preserves coherence while encouraging thoughtful experimentation. This understanding also reshapes the relationship between academic freedom and institutional identity.

Artificial intelligence has been discussed at times as though institutions must choose between these two values. Either faculty retain complete autonomy regarding AI use, or institutions establish increasingly detailed policies intended to ensure consistency. In practice, neither approach adequately serves the educational mission.

Academic freedom has never implied the absence of shared educational commitments. Faculty exercise considerable independence in selecting readings, designing assignments, and shaping classroom experiences, yet they do so within curricula that reflect collectively determined learning outcomes, disciplinary standards, and institutional purposes. Educational coherence has always depended upon this balance between individual judgment and shared responsibility.

An architectural university strengthens rather than weakens that balance. Faculty continue exercising professional judgment because they remain the individuals best positioned to understand the developmental needs of their disciplines and students. At the same time, their decisions become part of a larger educational conversation. AI-CAM levels, learning outcomes, assessment practices, and institutional policies provide a common vocabulary through which individual decisions can be understood within the broader developmental logic of the curriculum. Coherence emerges through shared educational purpose rather than administrative uniformity.

This shared purpose also changes how institutions understand innovation. Higher education has often measured innovation by novelty. New instructional technologies, redesigned classrooms, revised delivery models, and emerging pedagogical approaches are often presented as evidence that an institution is effectively preparing for the future. While innovation remains essential, architecture sets a higher standard.

The most important educational innovations are not necessarily those that introduce the newest technologies. They are those that strengthen the institution's ability to fulfill its mission under changing conditions.

Sometimes that will involve major technological integration. At other times, it may involve reaffirming the importance of independent inquiry, close reading, laboratory practice, clinical observation, or face-to-face dialogue. Architecture does not privilege innovation for its own sake. It asks whether any proposed change contributes meaningfully to students' long-term development. Seen in this way, artificial intelligence becomes neither an institutional threat nor an institutional identity.

It becomes one of many resources through which universities pursue their educational mission. There will undoubtedly be disciplines, programs, and courses in which AI assumes a significant instructional role. There will be others where its role remains intentionally limited. Both decisions may represent equally thoughtful educational design because the question has never been how much AI to incorporate into a curriculum. The question has always been what best serves student development at a particular stage of learning.

Perhaps nowhere is this architectural perspective more evident than in the role of the faculty.

Throughout the history of higher education, technological change has often raised concern that faculty members' importance would gradually diminish as new tools assumed responsibilities once carried out exclusively by instructors. Similar predictions accompanied correspondence education, instructional television, personal computing, online learning, and digital course management systems. While each innovation altered aspects of academic work, none diminished the university's need for thoughtful educators. Instead, faculty responsibilities evolved toward the areas where human judgment remained indispensable.

Artificial intelligence appears likely to continue that pattern. As routine instructional tasks are increasingly supported by intelligent technologies, the faculty member's distinctive contribution becomes even more clearly defined. Faculty remain responsible for cultivating disciplinary judgment, interpreting complexity, mentoring intellectual development, guiding ethical reasoning, and helping students integrate knowledge into coherent habits of professional practice. These responsibilities cannot be reduced to the efficient delivery of information because they concern the formation of persons rather than the transmission of content.

The architectural university, therefore, understands faculty less as distributors of knowledge than as stewards of learning environments.

Their expertise is expressed not only in what they know, but also in the educational experiences they intentionally design. They create conditions in which students learn to think carefully, question responsibly, evaluate critically, and exercise sound judgment within increasingly complex professional and cultural environments. Artificial intelligence may support many aspects of those environments, but it cannot replace the wisdom required to design them well.

This vision also reshapes how students experience higher education. Rather than encountering a collection of unrelated courses, they begin to recognize a developmental journey. Expectations become progressively more demanding because each stage builds intentionally upon those that preceded it. Independent performance prepares them for responsible collaboration. Collaboration prepares them for professional judgment. Professional judgment prepares them for leadership within increasingly complex organizations and communities. Students gradually discover that the curriculum has been designed not merely to help them complete courses, but to help them become the kind of professionals their disciplines require. That may be the clearest measure of an architectural university.

Its graduates leave with more than accumulated knowledge or technical proficiency. They possess a way of thinking that enables them to continue learning as professions, technologies, and societies evolve. Because their education has been organized around enduring principles rather than temporary tools, they remain capable of exercising thoughtful judgment long after the specific technologies they encountered as students have become obsolete.

Such a university is not defined by artificial intelligence. It is defined by the enduring educational wisdom that allows it to place every technology in its proper relationship to the larger work of human learning.

That observation points toward one final consideration. If architecture ultimately exists to serve something beyond itself, then the enduring significance of higher education cannot rest solely on curriculum design. Architecture remains the means. The greater purpose has always been the formation of persons whose knowledge, judgment, and character equip them to serve the common good.

The Enduring Work of Higher Education

Every generation is tempted to believe that its educational challenges are unprecedented.

The technologies differ. The cultural pressures change. Professional expectations evolve. Universities continually encounter circumstances that previous generations could not have anticipated. It is therefore understandable that discussions surrounding artificial intelligence often carry a sense of exceptional urgency, as though higher education stands at a decisive crossroads unlike any it has previously faced.

There is truth in that observation. Artificial intelligence will undoubtedly reshape many aspects of teaching, scholarship, and professional practice in ways that are still difficult to anticipate fully. Yet history also encourages a measure of perspective. Universities have endured because they remained remarkably clear about the enduring purposes those changes were meant to serve.

If the educational mission were merely the efficient transmission of information, the future of higher education would indeed appear uncertain. Information has become increasingly abundant and accessible, and is generated by automated systems whose capabilities continue to expand at an extraordinary pace. Universities cannot hope to distinguish themselves simply by providing information more efficiently than the technologies now available to almost every student. Fortunately, that has never been their highest calling.

The university exists because knowledge alone has never been sufficient. Education has always involved the formation of judgment, the acquisition of information, the cultivation of wisdom, the development of competence, and the shaping of character alongside the mastery of disciplinary knowledge. Students enter higher education not simply to accumulate facts but to become people capable of exercising responsible judgment within families, professions, communities, and societies whose challenges rarely present themselves in simple or predictable forms.

Artificial intelligence does not diminish the importance of that work. If anything, it makes it more urgent.

As technologies become increasingly capable of generating plausible answers, the ability to ask discerning questions becomes even more valuable. As automated systems produce analyses with remarkable speed and sophistication, graduates must become more skilled at evaluating evidence, recognizing limitations, exercising ethical responsibility, and accepting accountability for decisions whose consequences cannot be delegated to machines. Professional excellence will depend less upon possessing information than upon knowing how to interpret, evaluate, and apply it wisely. Those capacities have always distinguished an educated person. They remain the central work of higher education today.

For that reason, I hope readers will resist the temptation to view AI-CAM primarily as a framework for responding to artificial intelligence. Its greater aspiration is to encourage a way of thinking about curriculum that begins with human development and allows every subsequent educational decision to flow from that starting point. Artificial intelligence provided the context in which the framework emerged, but the underlying principles belong to a much longer educational tradition. They reflect the conviction that learning is developmental, that curriculum should be intentionally designed, and that every instructional decision should serve the larger work of intellectual and moral formation.

That conviction also suggests a particular understanding of institutional leadership. Leadership in higher education has never consisted simply of responding effectively to external change. Its deeper responsibility is stewardship. Trustees, presidents, provosts, deans, faculty members, instructional designers, and department chairs each hold in trust something that does not ultimately belong to them. They inherit institutions shaped by generations of educators who understood that universities exist not merely to prepare graduates for employment but to prepare them for lives of thoughtful responsibility. Every generation receives that inheritance, interprets it within its own historical moment, and then passes it forward.

Artificial intelligence now becomes part of that stewardship.

The task is not to preserve higher education exactly as it has always existed, nor to reshape it to accommodate every emerging technological possibility. Faithful stewardship has always required both continuity and adaptation. Institutions remain true to their mission not by resisting change, but by ensuring that change serves purposes more enduring than itself. Every generation of educators must decide anew how best to cultivate disciplined minds, ethical character, professional competence, and intellectual curiosity within the circumstances it has inherited.

Our generation is no different. The specific technologies will change. They always have. The artificial intelligence systems available today will eventually be replaced by capabilities that are difficult to imagine today. New questions will emerge. New opportunities will appear. Future educators will undoubtedly confront challenges that make today's conversations seem remarkably limited by comparison.

If this book proves useful beyond the present moment, I hope it will not be because it anticipated the future of artificial intelligence with unusual accuracy. No book can accomplish that. I hope, instead, that it offers a way of thinking about educational design that remains useful precisely because it is grounded in principles more durable than any particular technology. Institutions that learn to think developmentally, design intentionally, and evaluate innovation through the lens of educational purpose will remain capable of responding wisely to changes none of us can yet foresee.

Architecture is not simply a method for organizing curriculum. It is an expression of stewardship. It reflects the belief that education deserves thoughtful design because students deserve thoughtful formation. It recognizes that every course, every assessment, every policy, and every institutional decision participates in the larger work of shaping the lives entrusted to our care.

The future of higher education will certainly include artificial intelligence. More importantly, it will continue to require educators whose wisdom exceeds the capabilities of the technologies they employ. It will require faculty who understand that information is not the same as understanding, that efficiency is not the same as formation, and that professional competence cannot be separated from ethical responsibility. It will require institutions that possess the courage to embrace useful innovation while remaining firmly rooted in the enduring purposes that have always distinguished higher education from every other educational enterprise.

Those purposes remain remarkably constant. Universities exist to cultivate truth with intellectual honesty, to prepare students for lives of responsible service, to strengthen the professions upon which society depends, and to form women and men whose judgment, integrity, and wisdom enable them to contribute faithfully to the common good.

Artificial intelligence changes many aspects of how that work is carried out. It does not change the work itself. That work remains the enduring vocation of higher education. Long after today's technologies have passed into history, universities will still gather students and teachers around questions that matter, disciplines that shape judgment, and communities that cultivate wisdom. That work has always been the university's highest calling. It remains so today.

Appendix A: Institutional Design Cases: Applying AI-CAM Across the Developmental Continuum

Introduction

Throughout Part II, each AI-CAM level was examined through three questions. First, what pedagogical logic makes this level developmentally appropriate? Second, what does successful implementation look like in course design, assessment, and disclosure? Third, how does this level typically fail when its educational purpose is misunderstood?

Those chapters intentionally emphasized principles over examples.

The seven cases that follow illustrate how faculty members in different institutional contexts translated the developmental principles of AI-CAM into actual course design decisions. They are drawn from patterns repeatedly observed in faculty development work across higher education and represent authentic educational challenges rather than idealized scenarios.

The cases in this appendix are fictionalized composites based on recurring problems encountered in faculty development and course-design work. Institutions, instructors, timelines, results, and quotations have been created or adapted for illustrative purposes and should not be interpreted as reported research findings. These cases are not intended to serve as templates to be copied wholesale.

Curriculum architecture is always contextual. Institutional mission, disciplinary expectations, student preparation, accreditation requirements, and faculty judgment all shape appropriate implementation. A strategy that is entirely appropriate in one setting may be educationally inappropriate in another.

For that reason, the value of these cases lies less in their specific instructional choices than in the reasoning that produced those choices. Each illustrates how faculty identified a developmental problem, selected an appropriate AI-CAM level, aligned assignments and assessment with that level, responded to implementation challenges, and reflected on the educational results.

Readers should therefore approach these cases by asking not, *"How can I replicate this course?"* but rather, *"What design principles can I adapt within my own disciplinary and institutional context?"*

That question reflects the central conviction of this book.

Artificial intelligence is not integrated because a particular technology is available.

It is integrated because a specific stage of learning requires it.

The cases that follow demonstrate what that principle looks like when it is translated from curriculum theory into classroom practice.

Case 1 Preserving Foundational Learning – AI-CAM Level 0

First-Year Composition at a Regional Comprehensive University

At a mid-sized regional comprehensive university serving a largely first-generation student population, an instructor in the writing program faced a recurring challenge: incoming students arrived with dramatically uneven writing preparation, and the program's placement assessments were no longer providing reliable baseline data. Diagnostic essays were submitted with polished surface-level prose that masked gaps in argumentation, use of evidence, and analytical reasoning. After investigating, the instructor confirmed what colleagues across the department suspected – a substantial portion of students were using AI tools to revise or substantially rewrite their diagnostic submissions before turning them in.

The instructor redesigned the course's first four weeks as an explicit Level 0 environment. This was not announced as a punitive measure. In the revised syllabus, the instructor included a two-paragraph explanation of purpose: the restricted period existed to establish an honest baseline, to give students an accurate picture of their own current abilities, and to give the instructor the information needed to actually teach each student rather than a polished AI-assisted version of them. The framing mattered. Students who understood the diagnostic purpose of Level 0 were demonstrably more cooperative than those who experienced restriction as distrust.

Assignment Design

The centerpiece assignment of the Level 0 period was a three-stage in-class writing sequence. In the first session, students wrote an unassisted 600-word analytical response to a short reading completed as homework. No devices were permitted beyond printed materials. In the second session, one week later, students received their first draft back with only margin comments – no grades, no corrective edits – and spent 50 minutes revising in class. In the third session, students wrote a brief metacognitive reflection: What did you notice about your own draft? What was harder to revise than you expected? What questions do you still have about argument structure?

The sequence was designed to make the cognitive process visible rather than hiding it behind the product. The in-class constraint was not about preventing cheating – it was about creating conditions in which students could observe themselves thinking, struggling, and revising. That observational data, for both instructor and student, was the point.

Assessment Approach

The Level 0 sequence was assessed on a credit/no-credit basis with a single criterion: evidence of genuine engagement with the revision process. Students who produced a meaningfully different second draft – not necessarily a better one in surface terms, but one that showed they had grappled with their own first draft – received full credit. The metacognitive reflection was read but not graded. Its function was diagnostic, not evaluative.

At the end of week four, the instructor held brief individual conferences – eight minutes each – using the in-class writing sequence as the basis for a direct conversation: Here is what I see in your writing. Here is what we are going to work on. This conference was possible precisely because the Level 0 sequence had generated honest, unmediated writing samples. Without the AI restriction, the instructor would have been conferencing about polished surfaces rather than actual developmental needs.

Challenges Encountered

The most significant challenge was not student resistance – most students accepted the rationale when it was explained clearly – but instructor discomfort with the starkness of some results. When students who had been producing strong diagnostic essays for years suddenly struggled in class, the program had to confront what that gap actually meant. Several students who had appeared college-ready in placement were, under Level 0 conditions, demonstrably underprepared. This was uncomfortable institutional information that the Level 0 design made unavoidable.

A secondary challenge involved students with documented disabilities requiring extended time or assistive technology. The instructor worked with the disability services office to develop accommodations that preserved the diagnostic intent while meeting legal obligations – extended time in a separate supervised setting, with the same no-AI constraint applied consistently.

Faculty Reflection

Looking back on the redesign, the instructor noted that Level 0 had functioned less as a restriction and more as a diagnostic instrument. The absence of AI had not been the point in itself. The point was what that absence revealed. Students who knew their own writing – who had developed a working relationship with their own thinking process – were not disadvantaged by the restriction. Students who had come to depend on AI assistance for revision showed a different pattern: strong structure, weak reasoning, polished transitions between underdeveloped claims.

That pattern became the organizing insight of the course. Level 0 had not simply protected foundational skills. It had made visible exactly which foundational skills needed the most deliberate cultivation – and it had done so in the first four weeks, when there was still time to address them.

Level 0 Design Principles Illustrated in This Case

- Transparent rationale: Students understood the diagnostic purpose, not just the rule.
- Restriction as instrument: The constraint generated information, not just compliance.
- Assessment aligned with purpose: Credit/no-credit removed grade anxiety from the diagnostic process.
- Accommodation planning: Disability services integration preserved intent while meeting legal obligations.
- Defined exit point: Level 0 was explicitly temporary, with a clear transition to Level 1 in week five.

Case 2 Building a Culture of Transparency – AI-CAM Level 1

Introduction to Theology at a Faith-Based Liberal Arts College

At a small faith-based liberal arts college, a theology instructor teaching an introductory course to first- and second-year students faced a question that had become urgent across the institution: how to acknowledge the reality of AI tool use without either endorsing uncritical dependence or retreating into prohibition. The institution had not yet adopted a formal AI policy. The theology department had no shared guidance. The instructor was, in effect, designing a response to an institutional vacuum.

The course – Introduction to Systematic Theology – was not a writing-intensive course in the traditional sense, but it required students to engage original theological sources, construct arguments about doctrinal positions, and demonstrate familiarity with the interpretive traditions of the discipline. The instructor was concerned less with AI-generated prose than with AI-generated theological reasoning: students using language models to produce summaries of Aquinas or Augustine that appeared engaged without any actual encounter with the text.

Level 1 offered a workable middle path. AI tools were permitted. Their use had to be disclosed. The disclosure requirement, the instructor reasoned, would do more than ensure transparency – it would make students' relationship with the tools conscious rather than habitual.

Assignment Design

The instructor developed a standardized AI Disclosure Statement that accompanied every written assignment in the course. The form asked three questions: (1) Did you use an AI tool in completing this assignment? If so, which one? (2) For what specific purposes did you use it – summarizing a source, checking grammar, generating an outline, something else? (3) Did any AI-generated content appear, in modified or unmodified form, in your final submission? If so, identify where.

The form was one page, attached as the final page of every submission. Early in the semester, the instructor devoted twenty minutes of class time to a discussion of the form itself. Why these three questions? What distinguishes using AI to summarize a secondary source from using it to summarize a primary text you haven't read? Students engaged the distinction seriously – more seriously, the instructor noted, than they had engaged the course's academic integrity policy, which had been a paragraph in the syllabus none of them remembered.

The disclosure requirement also created an unexpected pedagogical opportunity. When a student disclosed that she had used an AI tool to generate an outline for her paper on the doctrine of grace, the instructor was able to ask: what did the AI's outline assume about the relationship between grace and human freedom? How does that assumption compare to Augustine's position? The disclosed use became a point of theological inquiry rather than a compliance matter.

Assessment Approach

Assignments were assessed on disciplinary criteria – quality of argument, accuracy of source engagement, clarity of theological reasoning – with one additional criterion added to the rubric: Source Transparency. This criterion did not penalize AI use. It assessed whether the student had accurately and completely disclosed their AI engagement. A student who used AI extensively but disclosed thoroughly received full marks on that criterion. A student who used AI but disclosed incompletely or inaccurately did not.

The practical effect was to make disclosure a positive act rather than a confession. Students were not hiding use and hoping not to be caught. They were documenting use as a professional practice – one that, the instructor repeatedly noted, mirrors how AI use is increasingly expected to be handled in theological scholarship, legal practice, journalism, and medicine.

Challenges Encountered

The most substantive challenge was definitional. Students were uncertain about where AI use began. Did using a grammar-checking tool constitute AI use requiring disclosure? What about the autocomplete function in their word processor? The instructor resolved this with a working definition: any tool that generates, summarizes, paraphrases, or evaluates substantive content requires disclosure. Tools that check spelling or suggest single-word replacements do not. Although imperfect at the margins, this boundary proved workable in practice.

A second challenge involved citation format. No established theological style guide had yet incorporated AI citation standards. The instructor developed a departmental template based on emerging APA guidance and shared it with colleagues – inadvertently beginning a departmental conversation about shared AI norms that the institution had not yet formally initiated.

Faculty Reflection

What surprised the instructor most was how the disclosure requirement changed not just transparency but engagement. Students who knew they would have to explain their AI use approached the tools differently. They were more deliberate. They used AI less reflexively and more strategically. Several students reported that completing the disclosure form had caused them to reconsider whether they needed to use the tool at all – and in some cases, to go back to the primary source instead.

Level 1 had not eliminated AI use. It had made that use conscious. And in a discipline whose entire intellectual tradition is built on the careful, accountable reading of texts, that shift from habitual to intentional was, the instructor reflected, already a form of theological formation.

Level 1 Design Principles Illustrated in This Case

- Disclosure as pedagogy: The three-question form generated classroom discussion, not just compliance records.

- Rubric integration: Source Transparency was a graded criterion – disclosure was valued, not just required.

• Definitional clarity: A working definition of 'AI use' reduced ambiguity without requiring exhaustive rules.

• Institutional ripple: One instructor's Level 1 design prompted a departmental policy conversation.

• Disciplinary fit: The disclosure requirement connected directly to the interpretive ethics of theological scholarship.

Case 3 AI as Learning Support — AI-CAM Level 2

Pathophysiology in a Community College Nursing Program

In a community college nursing program, an instructor teaching Pathophysiology to second-year students recognized a persistent pattern: students were spending disproportionate time organizing and summarizing dense textbook content, leaving insufficient time for the higher-order clinical reasoning the course was designed to develop. The cognitive load of content management was crowding out the cognitive work that mattered most for patient care.

The instructor had watched students produce beautifully organized notes on the pathophysiology of heart failure – accurate, comprehensive, well-formatted – and then struggle to answer a clinical scenario question requiring them to apply that content to a patient presentation. The organizational work was consuming time and energy that should have been available for application and analysis. AI tools, the instructor reasoned, could absorb the organizational load if students were given explicit permission and guidance to use them for that purpose – freeing cognitive resources for the clinical reasoning tasks that AI could not perform.

The course was redesigned at Level 2 with a specific framing: AI is permitted and encouraged for content organization, study guide generation, and initial concept summarization. It is not permitted as a substitute for clinical reasoning, scenario analysis, or any graded assessment unless explicitly noted. The distinction was not arbitrary. It was grounded in a clear model of where human judgment was irreplaceable in nursing practice.

Assignment Design

The centerpiece of the Level 2 redesign was a two-stage preparation structure for each unit. In stage one, students were explicitly encouraged to use AI tools to generate a structured concept summary of the assigned pathophysiology content – mechanism of disease, clinical presentation, diagnostic indicators, and treatment principles. Students were required to review, correct, and annotate the AI-generated summary before bringing it to class. The annotation requirement was non-negotiable: every AI-generated claim had to be verified against the course textbook or a peer-reviewed source, with the verification noted in the margin.

In stage two, class time was restructured around clinical scenario analysis – complex patient presentations that required students to apply the content from stage one to real-world decision-making. The scenarios were designed to be unsolvable by AI summarization. They required synthesis across multiple body systems, attention to complicating factors like age, comorbidities, and medication interactions, and the kind of probabilistic clinical reasoning that characterizes actual nursing judgment.

The AI-generated summaries from stage one were permitted in the room during scenario work. They functioned as reference material – a scaffold that freed students from retrieval tasks so they could focus on application. The instructor described this explicitly to students: 'I am not interested in whether you can recall the ejection fraction threshold for heart failure. I am interested in whether you can recognize what it means when you are standing at a patient's bedside.'

Assessment Approach

The stage-one concept summaries were assessed on two dimensions: accuracy (verified against textbook content) and annotation quality (did the student's annotations demonstrate genuine engagement with the AI output, or were they perfunctory checkmarks?). Summaries with substantive annotations – questions the student had, corrections to AI errors, connections the student had drawn between concepts – received full credit. Summaries with minimal or absent annotation received partial credit regardless of their surface quality.

The clinical scenarios were assessed independently, without reference to the AI-generated summaries, using a clinical reasoning rubric that evaluated patient data recognition, differential reasoning, intervention prioritization, and safety awareness. This separation was intentional: the assessment of clinical reasoning could not be contaminated by the quality of the AI summary. The two dimensions needed to be evaluated independently to yield meaningful information about what each student could actually do.

Challenges Encountered

An early challenge was annotation quality. Students interpreted the annotation requirement as a fact-checking exercise – a binary yes/no for each claim – rather than an exercise in engagement. The instructor responded by developing a set of annotation prompts: What does this claim assume about normal physiology? What patient population might present differently? What is the clinical implication of this mechanism? These prompts transformed annotation from compliance into genuine cognitive work.

A second challenge involved AI accuracy. In one unit on renal pathophysiology, multiple students submitted AI-generated summaries that contained a subtle but clinically significant error in their descriptions of the renin-angiotensin-aldosterone system. The error was consistent across students, suggesting they had used similar prompts and received similar outputs. The instructor turned this into a class discussion: here is what the AI got wrong, here is why it matters clinically, here is how you would catch it. The error became one of the most memorable teaching moments of the semester.

Faculty Reflection

The results of the redesign were measurable. Clinical scenario performance — the assessment most directly linked to actual nursing competence — improved meaningfully compared to the prior cohort. The instructor attributed this not to the AI tools themselves but to the cognitive reallocation they enabled. When students were no longer spending three hours building content summaries from scratch, they had three additional hours for scenario practice, faculty office hours, and the kind of slow, deliberate reasoning that clinical competence requires.

The instructor also noted an unexpected benefit: AI errors had become a teaching resource. The regularity with which AI tools produced confident, plausible, and clinically wrong information about pharmacology and pathophysiology had given the course a new and concrete way to teach critical evaluation of sources. Students who had learned to annotate AI summaries with genuine skepticism were, the instructor observed, also becoming more skeptical readers of clinical guidelines, research abstracts, and the confident pronouncements of senior colleagues — which is precisely the disposition a safe nurse needs.

Level 2 Design Principles Illustrated in This Case

- Purposeful permission: AI use was encouraged for a specific cognitive task, not for everything.

- Annotation as engagement: The verification requirement transformed summarization from passive to active.

- Cognitive reallocation: Offloading organization to AI freed students for higher-order clinical reasoning.

- Error as pedagogy: AI inaccuracies became teaching material rather than problems to hide.

- Assessment separation: AI-supported preparation and independent reasoning were assessed independently.

Case 4 Learning to Critique AI – AI-CAM Level 3

Research Methods in Sociology at a Large Public University

At a large public research university, an instructor teaching upper-division Research Methods in Sociology had long struggled with a specific pedagogical problem: students understood research methodology in the abstract but had difficulty recognizing methodological strengths and limitations in real research contexts. They could define sampling bias on an exam. They could not reliably identify it when reading a news article that cited a survey.

The instructor saw an opportunity in AI's well-documented tendency to produce methodologically confident but often flawed research summaries. Large language models, when prompted to describe or summarize research findings, frequently flatten nuance, omit limitations, overstate generalizability, and present correlational findings in causal language. These are precisely the methodological errors that sociologists are trained to identify. The AI's weaknesses, the instructor realized, were pedagogically useful – if students were required to engage them critically rather than accept them uncritically.

The course was redesigned to include one required AI-engagement assignment midway through the semester. The assignment was not optional, and its purpose was stated explicitly in the syllabus: students would use AI as a subject of methodological analysis, not as a research assistant.

Assignment Design

The assignment – titled the AI Methodological Audit – unfolded in three stages over two weeks. In stage one, each student selected a published sociological study from the course reading list and submitted a structured prompt to an AI tool asking it to summarize the study's findings, methodology, and limitations. Students submitted both the prompt they used and the complete AI-generated response as part of their assignment.

In stage two, students conducted a systematic methodological audit of the AI's response using a framework developed in class: seven evaluative categories drawn directly from the course's methodology curriculum. These categories included sampling and generalizability, operationalization of key variables, causal versus correlational claims, treatment of competing explanations, acknowledgment of researcher positionality, representation of the study's own stated limitations, and accuracy of statistical interpretation. For each category, students rated the AI response on a three-point scale and provided a written justification citing specific language from both the AI response and the original study.

In stage three, students wrote a 600-word synthesis: Given what you found in your audit, under what conditions – if any – would you use this AI tool as a research aid in a sociological research project? What safeguards would be necessary? This synthesis question required students to move from evaluation to professional judgment – the metacognitive step that transformed the assignment from a critique exercise into a genuine professional formation experience.

Assessment Approach

The assignment was assessed using a rubric with four weighted criteria. Prompt Construction (15%) evaluated whether the student's initial prompt was specific, appropriately scoped, and likely to generate useful output – rewarding the skill of effective AI engagement rather than treating prompt quality as irrelevant. Audit Accuracy (40%) evaluated the correctness and completeness of the methodological audit, assessed against the instructor's own audit of the same AI responses. Evidence Use (25%) evaluated whether students cited specific textual evidence from both the AI response and the original study rather than making general claims. Professional Synthesis (20%) evaluated the quality of reasoning in the stage-three reflection.

The rubric made visible a distinction the course had struggled to assess clearly in previous years: the difference between students who understood methodology as a set of definitions and students who could apply methodological reasoning to unfamiliar material. The AI

Methodological Audit required the latter. Students who had memorized the course's methodological vocabulary without internalizing the reasoning behind it performed poorly on audit accuracy — not because the AI had tricked them, but because genuine methodological evaluation requires genuine methodological understanding.

Challenges Encountered

The most substantive challenge was variability in AI output. Because students used different tools and prompts, and prompted the same tool on different days, the AI responses they audited varied considerably in quality. Some students received AI summaries that were largely accurate. Others received summaries with numerous errors. This variability was educationally productive in some ways — students had to develop their own judgment rather than grading against a single standard — but it complicated the assessment of audit accuracy, since the instructor had to evaluate each student's audit against the specific AI response that student had received.

The instructor addressed this by requiring students to submit the complete AI response as part of their assignment and by spending additional time preparing to review a sample of AI outputs before grading. This added assessment burden was real, but the instructor concluded, unavoidable if the assignment was to remain authentic. Standardizing the AI output by providing students with a pre-generated response would have eliminated the variability, but also eliminated the professional skill of working with unpredictable tool behavior, which is the actual condition under which sociologists will encounter these tools in practice.

Faculty Reflection

End-of-semester evaluations showed that the AI Methodological Audit was the assignment students most frequently cited as changing how they thought about research methods. Several students noted that auditing an AI response had taught them more about sampling bias than any lecture or reading had, because the AI's errors had been vivid and concrete rather than abstract and hypothetical.

The instructor drew a broader conclusion from the experience: AI tools are, in disciplines with rigorous methodological traditions, an almost ideal subject of critical analysis. Their errors are systematic, their overconfidence is consistent, and their limitations mirror precisely the methodological weaknesses that disciplinary training is designed to correct. At Level 3, the AI had not been a research assistant. It had been a research subject – and a highly instructive one.

Level 3 Design Principles Illustrated in This Case

- AI as subject, not assistant: The tool's limitations were the pedagogical content, not obstacles to it.

- Staged structure: Three stages moved students from prompt construction through audit to professional synthesis.

- Rubric transparency: Prompt Construction was a graded criterion, signaling that AI engagement is a skill.

- Productive variability: Inconsistent AI outputs were treated as authentic professional conditions, not problems.

- Metacognitive capstone: The synthesis question required judgment, not just evaluation.

Case 5 AI Literacy as a Learning Outcome — AI-CAM Level 4

Business Strategy in an MBA Program

At a private university's MBA program, the curriculum committee had spent two years discussing whether and how to formalize AI literacy as a program-level competency. The conversation had repeatedly stalled on the same question: Which courses should carry AI literacy outcomes? How do you assess a competency that cuts across tools, disciplines, and professional contexts? Who is responsible for teaching it?

Rather than waiting for program-level consensus, an instructor teaching the required second-year Business Strategy course proposed a pilot: embed explicit, measurable AI literacy outcomes directly into the course's existing learning objectives, design assignments that assessed those outcomes alongside disciplinary content, and report results to the curriculum committee as evidence for the broader program conversation. The proposal was approved. The course became the program's first intentional Level 4 implementation.

The course's existing learning outcomes were strong. Students were expected to conduct competitive analysis, develop strategic recommendations, evaluate organizational capabilities, and communicate strategic reasoning to senior stakeholders. The instructor did not replace these outcomes. She added four AI literacy competencies that intersected directly with each of them: (1) the ability to use AI tools to accelerate environmental scanning and competitive intelligence gathering; (2) the ability to identify and correct AI-generated distortions in strategic data; (3) the ability to document and justify AI-assisted analytical decisions; and (4) the ability to articulate the ethical implications of AI deployment as a strategic tool within organizations.

Assignment Design

The course's signature assignment – a Strategic Analysis Project completed in teams of three over the final eight weeks – was redesigned to incorporate AI literacy at every stage. Teams were required to use at least two AI tools during the competitive analysis phase and to maintain an AI Decision Log throughout: a structured document recording which tools were used, what prompts were submitted, what outputs were generated, which outputs were used and which were discarded, and why.

The AI Decision Log was not a bureaucratic requirement. It was a professional document modeled on the analytical audit trails that strategy consultants maintain to demonstrate the rigor of their process to clients. The instructor framed it explicitly this way: in the professional environments you are entering, you will be asked to defend not just your conclusions but your analytical process. The AI Decision Log is practice for that accountability.

The final deliverable — a strategic recommendation memorandum addressed to a fictional executive team — was required to include a one-page AI Methodology Appendix summarizing how AI tools had been used in the analysis, what their limitations had been in that specific context, and what human analytical judgment had been required to supplement or correct the AI-generated work. This appendix was assessed separately from the memo's strategic content.

Assessment Approach

The rubric for the Strategic Analysis Project included six criteria. Three assessed disciplinary mastery: analytical depth, strategic coherence of recommendations, and quality of stakeholder communication. Three assessed AI literacy: accuracy and completeness of the AI Decision Log, quality of the AI Methodology Appendix, and evidence in the final memo that AI-generated content had been critically evaluated rather than uncritically adopted.

The separation of criteria was deliberate and, early in the semester, controversial. Several students objected that they were being graded on process documentation as well as analytical quality. The instructor's response became one of the course's recurring themes: in strategy work, the process is part of the product. An analysis that cannot be explained and defended is not a finished analysis. An AI-assisted conclusion that cannot be traced back through a documented analytical chain is not a defensible recommendation. The objection and its response became a productive framework for the course's broader discussion of professional accountability in AI-mediated environments.

Challenges Encountered

The most significant challenge was team dynamics around AI use. Within several teams, one member was more fluent with AI tools than the others. In a few cases, this fluency differential led to an informal division of labor in which the AI-fluent member handled all tool interaction while teammates focused on other aspects of the project – an arrangement that satisfied no one's learning needs and produced AI Decision Logs that reflected the work of one person rather than three.

The instructor addressed this mid-semester by requiring each team member to submit an individual AI Reflection – a brief personal account of how they had personally engaged with AI tools during the project, separate from the team's shared documentation. The individual reflection broke the division-of-labor dynamic by making each student personally accountable for their own AI engagement. It also surfaced important differences in confidence and fluency that the instructor addressed in office hours before the final submission.

Faculty Reflection

At the end of the semester, the instructor presented findings to the curriculum committee. Student performance on the AI literacy criteria had been stronger than expected: the AI Methodology Appendix, which the instructor had anticipated would be the weakest component, was consistently thoughtful and often more candid about AI limitations than the students' disciplinary analyses. Students, it turned out, were more willing to acknowledge uncertainty about AI tools than uncertainty about their own strategic judgment.

The curriculum committee voted to expand Level 4 implementation to three additional required courses in the following year. The instructor's framing of AI literacy as an extension of professional accountability – rather than a separate technical competency – had provided the conceptual bridge that two years of abstract policy discussion had failed to build.

Level 4 Design Principles Illustrated in This Case

- Outcome integration: AI literacy competencies were added to, not substituted for, existing disciplinary outcomes.

- Professional framing: The AI Decision Log was modeled on actual consulting practice, not invented for the course.

- Rubric transparency: AI literacy criteria carried equal weight to disciplinary criteria – signaling genuine priority.

- Individual accountability: Individual reflections within team projects prevented fluency-based division of labor.

- Institutional leverage: Pilot data from one course provided evidence for program-level curriculum change.

Case 6 Learning Through Structured AI Collaboration – AI-CAM Level 5

MFA Creative Writing Workshop

The creative writing workshop was perhaps the last place most faculty in the program expected to encounter structured AI integration. The discipline's resistance to AI tools had been pronounced and, in many cases, principled: creative writing programs exist precisely to cultivate individual voice, aesthetic judgment, and the kind of irreducibly personal creative risk-taking that no tool can replicate. The argument for prohibition was not reactionary. It was grounded in a coherent theory of what creative development requires.

The instructor of the Advanced Fiction Workshop was not unsympathetic to that argument. But she had also observed something troubling in her students' relationship with revision: they had become reluctant to destabilize their own drafts. Advanced MFA students, she had noticed, produced technically accomplished prose that rarely surprised them. They were writing within the limits of what they already knew they could do. Revision had become refinement rather than transformation.

She designed a Level 5 integration not to generate student writing but to generate productive creative friction — to use AI as a collaborator whose responses to a draft would be genuinely alien to the student's own aesthetic sensibility, and therefore potentially generative of unexpected creative directions. AI collaboration was not a shortcut. It was a deliberate disruption of a creative comfort zone.

Assignment Design

The assignment structure — called the Dialogue Draft — unfolded over four weeks. In week one, students submitted a completed short story draft, approximately 3,000 words, to the workshop in the traditional format. Workshop discussion proceeded as usual.

In week two, each student conducted three structured AI collaboration sessions with their draft. The sessions were not open-ended. The instructor provided specific prompt frameworks for each session: In session one, students asked the AI to identify the story's implicit assumptions about its protagonist — what the narrative took for granted about the character that the character might dispute. In session two, students asked the AI to rewrite the story's climactic scene from the perspective of the character the narrative treated most superficially. In session three, students asked the AI to identify three structural choices in the story — not stylistic ones, but architectural ones about what happens when, to whom, and in what order — and to propose alternative structures with brief rationales.

Students were required to submit transcripts for all three AI sessions along with their reflection. In week three, they submitted a substantially revised draft — not a polished revision, but an exploratory one that showed evidence of genuine engagement with the AI collaboration. The revision did not need to incorporate any specific AI suggestion. It needed to demonstrate that the collaboration had generated new creative thinking, whatever form that took. In week four, the class workshopped the revised drafts alongside the AI session transcripts, openly discussing what the AI collaboration had and had not contributed.

Assessment Approach

Assessment of the Dialogue Draft was organized around two independent evaluations. The revised draft was evaluated on standard workshop criteria: narrative coherence, character development, prose control, thematic complexity, and evidence of meaningful revision from draft one to draft two. The AI collaboration transcript and the accompanying student reflection were evaluated separately on three criteria: quality of the prompts (were they specific, purposeful, and generative?), evidence of critical engagement with the AI responses (did the student evaluate the AI's suggestions or simply note them?), and the relationship between the AI collaboration and the revision choices (could the student articulate, with specificity, how the collaboration had influenced their creative thinking – even where they had chosen to reject AI suggestions?).

The last criterion – articulating how the collaboration influenced creative thinking, including in rejection – was the most intellectually demanding. Students who had ignored the AI entirely could not meet it. Students who had accepted AI suggestions uncritically could not meet it either. It required a genuine, reflective account of collaborative creative process – which is, the instructor argued, precisely the kind of metacognitive awareness that separates developing writers from mature ones.

Challenges Encountered

The most honest challenge was instructor discomfort. Introducing AI into a creative writing workshop felt, to the instructor and to several colleagues, like a category violation – an intrusion of instrumental logic into a space that was supposed to be free of it. That discomfort was real and, the instructor concluded, not entirely wrong. It had to be held alongside the pedagogical rationale rather than resolved. The answer was not to pretend that AI collaboration was neutral or that the discipline had no legitimate concerns about it. The answer was to design the collaboration in a way that served the specific pedagogical purpose – disrupting creative comfort zones – while building in explicit critical reflection on the tool's limitations and the discipline's values.

A second challenge was student anxiety about voice contamination – the fear that engaging with AI-generated prose would degrade their own stylistic development. The instructor addressed this directly: your voice is not as fragile as you think. You read fiction written by other people every week and your prose does not become theirs. Engaging critically with AI-generated alternatives to your own choices is not categorically different. Several students remained skeptical. But those students also produced some of the most intellectually vigorous critical reflections in the class – because the discomfort had made them articulate, in precise terms, what they valued about their own creative practice. That articulation was itself a developmental outcome.

Faculty Reflection

The revision quality in the Dialogue Draft cohort was, by the instructor's assessment, the strongest she had seen in four years of teaching the course. Not because AI had improved the prose – it had not, directly – but because the structured collaboration had forced students into a more genuinely exploratory relationship with their own material. Several students produced revisions that surprised them. The AI's alien aesthetic sensibility had, in several cases, made visible creative possibilities that the students' own too-close relationship with their drafts had obscured.

The instructor was careful not to overstate the conclusion. Level 5 creative AI collaboration was not appropriate for all stages of development or all creative contexts. For beginning writers still developing foundational craft skills, the disruption might be more destabilizing than generative. For advanced students with established voices and the metacognitive capacity to evaluate the collaboration critically, it had opened creative doors. Context, developmental stage, and instructional intentionality were everything.

Level 5 Design Principles Illustrated in This Case

- Purposeful disruption: AI was used to generate creative friction, not creative content.
- Structured prompts: The three-session frameworks prevented open-ended, unfocused AI engagement.
- Dual assessment: The revised draft and the collaboration transcript were evaluated independently.
- Rejection as evidence: Articulating why AI suggestions were rejected was a valid and valued outcome.
- Disciplinary honesty: Instructor discomfort was acknowledged and held rather than resolved or suppressed.

Case 7 Designing an AI-Integrated Learning Environment — AI-CAM Level 6

Course Context: Applied Machine Learning in a Graduate Engineering Program

At a large research university, a graduate-level Applied Machine Learning course had been operating with a persistent structural tension: the course covered both theoretical foundations and applied implementation, but the wide variation in students' mathematical preparation meant that some students needed to spend focused time on foundational concepts while others were ready to move quickly to implementation. A single-paced lecture model served neither group well. Students who needed more time on mathematical prerequisites felt rushed. Students ready for advanced implementation felt held back. Formative assessment was occurring too late – at the midterm – to be actionable.

The instructor redesigned the Level 6 course over an 18-month period in collaboration with the university's instructional design office and IT infrastructure team. The redesign embedded AI tools into three distinct layers of the course architecture: an adaptive prerequisite scaffolding system, an AI-assisted code review and feedback loop, and a portfolio assessment platform that tracked student reasoning across the semester. Faculty retained full evaluative authority at every layer. AI generated feedback and flagged patterns. The instructor interpreted, contextualized, and made final judgments.

Assignment Design

The adaptive scaffolding layer operated in the first four weeks. Students completed a diagnostic assessment in week one that evaluated mathematical prerequisites across six domains: linear algebra, calculus, probability theory, statistics, Python fluency, and algorithmic thinking. The AI system analyzed diagnostic results and generated individualized reading and exercise sequences for each student – drawing from a curated library of resources the instructor had pre-approved and organized by difficulty level. Students were not tracked into different courses. They were given differentiated on-ramps to the same course. The instructor reviewed the system's recommendations for each student before they were released, overriding in several cases where the diagnostic had misclassified a student's preparation level.

The AI-assisted code review layer operated throughout the semester. When students submitted programming assignments – implementing algorithms, training models, conducting experiments – the AI system provided an initial technical feedback report within two hours of submission: syntax errors, efficiency issues, and flagged sections where the code's logic appeared inconsistent with the student's stated methodology. Crucially, the system did not provide corrected code. It identified issues and asked questions. 'Your loss function implementation differs from the one described in your methodology section. Was this intentional?' Students were required to respond to flagged items before the instructor reviewed the submission, creating a two-stage process in which the AI handled pattern recognition and the instructor handled evaluation of reasoning and judgment.

The portfolio platform accumulated student work across the semester and generated weekly summary reports for the instructor: which students had engaged with prerequisite scaffolding, which had not; which code review flags had been resolved substantively versus superficially; which students showed a pattern of addressing surface-level issues while avoiding deeper conceptual ones. The instructor used these reports to target office hours conversations and to identify students who needed direct intervention before problems compounded.

Assessment Approach

The course's final assessment was a Capstone Technical Report — an original machine learning project in which students defined a problem, selected and justified an approach, implemented a solution, evaluated results, and reflected on limitations. The AI system played no direct role in evaluating the capstone. It was assessed by the instructor and, for students proposing to submit it for conference consideration, by an external reviewer.

The semester's process data — prerequisite engagement, code review response patterns, portfolio summaries — were not factored directly into the capstone grade. They informed the instructor's understanding of each student's development, but did not mechanically weight the final assessment. The instructor's explicit rationale: AI-generated process data should inform judgment, not replace it. A student who had struggled early but demonstrated clear, positive development by the capstone deserved to be assessed on the capstone, not penalized by automated tracking of early struggles.

The Role of Faculty Presence

The course's most significant finding — and the one most relevant to other institutions considering Level 6 implementation — had nothing to do with the technology. It concerned the relationship between AI-mediated feedback and instructor-mediated human contact.

Student satisfaction data collected at mid-semester showed a strong correlation between students' perception of the AI feedback systems and the quality of their weekly synchronous sessions with the instructor. Students who found the weekly sessions clarifying, responsive, and personally engaged rated the AI feedback tools as highly effective. Students who found the weekly sessions impersonal, rushed, or poorly connected to the course's AI-generated reports rated the same tools as frustrating and insufficient.

The AI systems had not changed. The instruction had. What determined whether the AI architecture felt like a supportive ecosystem or an impersonal machine was the quality of the human relationship into which it was embedded. Students could tolerate – and even appreciate – the efficiency and scale of AI-generated feedback when they trusted that a human instructor was monitoring their development, interpreting the patterns, and available to intervene. Without that trust, the same feedback felt like surveillance rather than support.

The instructor responded to mid-semester findings by restructuring the weekly sessions to open with a five-minute acknowledgment of patterns the AI reports had surfaced that week – normalizing the data, contextualizing it, and making visible the instructor's active role in interpreting it. This small structural change had a measurable effect on student satisfaction and, the instructor believed, on student willingness to engage genuinely with the AI feedback systems rather than managing them strategically.

Challenges Encountered

The implementation challenges at Level 6 were, predictably, the most complex of any level. Data privacy compliance required careful coordination with the university's legal and IT offices – the adaptive scaffolding system stored student performance data, which triggered FERPA considerations that took three months to resolve before the redesign could launch. The instructor also encountered resistance from two colleagues who argued that AI-generated code review feedback, however qualified, constituted a form of automated grading that violated shared governance norms about faculty control of assessment. This concern was addressed through a memorandum of clarification — formally adopted by the department's curriculum committee — that defined AI feedback tools as instructional scaffolding rather than assessment instruments, and reaffirmed that all grades were determined by faculty evaluation.

The technical maintenance burden was also higher than anticipated. When a third-party AI tool updated its underlying model mid-semester, the code review feedback shifted in ways that disoriented students who had learned to interpret the previous model's output patterns. The instructor spent a lot of time communicating the change, recalibrating expectations, and in two cases, reviewing earlier submissions that students felt had been assessed against inconsistent standards. This experience reinforced a design principle the instructor now considers non-negotiable: Level 6 implementations require institutional IT support, not just individual faculty effort. The complexity of maintaining an AI-integrated course architecture exceeds what a single instructor should be expected to manage alone.

Faculty Reflection

Three years after the initial redesign, the instructor offered a candid summary for colleagues considering Level 6 implementation: the technology had delivered on its promises in specific, bounded ways. Adaptive scaffolding had meaningfully reduced the preparation gap that had previously disadvantaged students from non-traditional mathematical backgrounds. AI-assisted code review had provided formative feedback at a scale and speed that was genuinely impossible through human grading alone. The portfolio platform had given the instructor information that had changed how she taught — not just how she assessed.

But the most important insight was one that could not have been predicted from the technology itself: Level 6 had not made the course less human. It had made the human elements more important, more visible, and more consequential. The architecture was sophisticated. The soul of the course was still a person who cared whether each student succeeded — and who was, because of the architecture, better informed about what each student needed than she had ever been before.

Level 6 Design Principles Illustrated in This Case

- Layered architecture: Three distinct AI systems served three distinct pedagogical functions.
- Faculty override: Instructor reviewed and modified AI recommendations before they reached students.
- Feedback without answers: AI flagged issues and asked questions – it did not provide corrections.
- Human correlation: Student perception of AI tools was strongly tied to quality of instructor presence.
- Institutional infrastructure: FERPA compliance and shared governance required formal institutional coordination.
- Technology maintenance: Mid-semester tool updates required active communication and re-calibration.

References:

Andrews, J., Chaudhuri, S., Kong, L., & Sarsfield, M. (2021). Book review—2021. *Journal of Interactive Media in Education, 2021*(1), Article 29, 1–9. https://doi.org/10.5334/jime.721

Baker, R. S., & Hawn, A. (2022). Algorithmic bias in education. *International Journal of Artificial Intelligence in Education, 32,* 1052–1092. https://doi.org/10.1007/s40593-021-00285-9

Bian, Q., Ling, X., & Yan, S. (2024). Bridging the algorithmic divide: Refocusing faculty artificial intelligence literacy in higher education. *Education as Change, 28,* 1-12. https://doi.org/10.25159/1947-9417/17983

Biggs, J. (1996). Enhancing teaching through constructive alignment. *Higher Education, 32*(3), 347–364. https://doi.org/10.1007/BF00138871

Blodgett, S. L., Barocas, S., Daumé, H., & Wallach, H. (2020). Language (technology) is power: A critical survey of "bias" in NLP. *Proceedings of the 58th Annual Meeting of the Association for Computational Linguistics,* 5454–5476. https://doi.org/10.18653/v1/2020.acl-main.485

Boud, D., & Dawson, P. (2023). What feedback literate teachers do: An empirically-derived competency framework. *Assessment & Evaluation in Higher Education, 48*(2), 158–171. https://doi-org.belhaven.idm.oclc.org/10.1080/02602938.2021.1910928

Chen, K., Tallant, A. C., & Selig, I. (2025). Exploring generative AI literacy in higher education: Student adoption, interaction, evaluation and ethical perceptions. *Information & Learning Science, 126*(1/2), 132–148. https://doi.org/10.1108/ILS-10-2023-0160

Civil Rights Act of 1964, 42 U.S.C. § 2000d.

Hargittai, E. (2002). Second-level digital divide: Differences in people's online skills. *First Monday, 7*(4). https://doi.org/10.5210/fm.v7i4.942

Kocdar, S. (2017). Teaching in a digital age: Guidelines for designing teaching and learning for a digital age. *International Review of Research in Open & Distributed Learning, 18*(3), 159–162. https://doi-org.belhaven.idm.oclc.org/10.19173/irrodl.v18i3.3107

Lo, C. K. (2023). What is the impact of ChatGPT on education? A rapid review of the literature. *Education Sciences, 13*(4), 410. https://doi.org/10.3390/educsci13040410

Medina-Gual, L., Medina-Velázquez, L., & Parejo, J.-L. (2025). A tridimensional model of AI literacy: An empirical analysis of student performance and demographic patterns in higher education. *Australasian Journal of Educational Technology, 41*(5), 37–55.

Perkins, M., Roe, J., Postma, D., McGaughran, J., & Hickerson, D. (2023). Detection of GPT-4 generated text in higher education: Combining academic judgement and software to identify generative AI tool misuse. *Journal of Academic Ethics, 22*(1), 89–113. https://doi.org/10.1007/s10805-023-09492-6

Rose, D. H., & Meyer, A. (2002). *Teaching every student in the digital age: Universal design for learning.* ASCD.

Moore, S. (2007). David H. Rose, Anne Meyer, Teaching every student in the digital age: Universal design for learning. In *Educational Technology Research & Development* (Vol. 55,

Issue 5, pp. 521–525). Springer Nature. https://doi-org.belhaven.idm.oclc.org/10.1007/s11423-007-9056-3

Sposato, M. (2025). Artificial intelligence in educational leadership: A comprehensive taxonomy and future directions. *International Journal of Educational Technology in Higher Education, 22*(1), 1–18. https://doi.org/10.1186/s41239-025-00517-1

Wiggins, G., (1990) "The Case for Authentic Assessment", *Practical Assessment, Research, and Evaluation* 2(1): 2. doi: https://doi.org/10.7275/ffb1-mm19

Yan, L., Sha, L., Zhao, L., Li, Y., Martinez-Maldonado, R., Chen, G., Li, X., Jin, Y., & Gasevic, D. (2024). Practical and ethical challenges of large language models in education: A systematic scoping review. *British Journal of Educational Technology, 55*(1), 90–112. https://doi.org/10.1111/bjet.13370

www.ingramcontent.com/pod-product-compliance
Lightning Source LLC
LaVergne TN
LVHW050808061126
851857LV00012B/728
* 9 7 8 2 2 9 6 0 0 9 7 6 9 *